MUSIC FOR EVENING PRAYER

Settings for Vespers throughout the year

Abbot Alan Rees

Kevin Mayhew

We hope you enjoy *Music for Evening Prayer*. Further copies are available from your local Kevin Mayhew stockist.

In case of difficulty, please contact the publisher direct by writing to:

The Sales Department
KEVIN MAYHEW LTD
Buxhall
Stowmarket
Suffolk IP14 3BW

Phone 01449 737978
Fax 01449 737834
E-mail info@kevinmayhewltd.com

Please ask for our complete catalogue of outstanding Church Music.

Acknowledgements

We wish to express our gratitude to The Grail (England) for permission to reproduce the Psalms from *The Grail Translation;* A. P. Watt Ltd, 20 John Street, London WC1N, for the Prayers and Canticles which are extracted from *The Divine Office,* © The Hierarchies of England & Wales, Ireland and Australia; and the Trustees of Downside Abbey for *Alma Redemptoris Mater* and *Salve, Regina* by Gregory Murray.

All the music in this book is by Alan Rees OSB unless indicated otherwise.

First published in Great Britain in 2001 by Kevin Mayhew Ltd.

© Copyright 2001 Kevin Mayhew Ltd.

ISBN 1 84003 805 5
ISMN M 57004 927 1
Catalogue No: 1450233

0 1 2 3 4 5 6 7 8 9

Cover design by Angela Selfe

Music setter: Donald Thomson
Proof reader: Marian Hellen

Printed and bound in Great Britain

Foreword

was the hope of the bishops in the Second Vatican Council that, in accordance with ancient custom, Vespers ould be celebrated with the people on Sundays and lemnities.

ome extracts from the General Instruction on the turgy of the Hours (GILH), will serve to underline e importance they attached to this:

¶1. The public and communal prayer of the people of God is rightly considered among the first duties of the Church.

¶40. In the prayer of the Christian community, Lauds (Morning Prayer) and Vespers (Evening Prayer) are of the highest importance. Their public and common celebration should be encouraged.

¶39. Vespers is celebrated in the evening when the day is drawing to a close, so that 'we may give thanks for what has been given us during the day, or for the things we have done well during it.'

¶246. Provided that the general arrangement of the Hour is maintained and that the rules which follow it are observed, texts other than those found in the Office of the day may be chosen on particular occasions.

¶247. In place of the Sunday psalms of the current week, the Sunday psalms of another week may be substituted if desired. Especially in the Office with the people, other psalms may be chosen so as gradually to bring the people to a deeper understanding of the psalms.

1 practice, this hope has been fulfilled in very few laces outside the Cathedral and Abbey churches. One f the reasons for this has been the unavailability of asier music settings of the English texts.

am glad to have the opportunity to share some melodies similar to those developed and used in the celebration of Vespers or Evening Prayer at Belmont Abbey over the past thirty years. Generally, these melodies are modally based and easy to sing, with a simple rgan accompaniment, sufficient to sustain the pitch. General directions with regard to the structure and manner of singing Evening Prayer will be found below.

he Intercessions are based on the work of Susan Sayers nd Frances Wood to whom I express my thanks.

pray that this publication will help the faithful to participate in the Evening Prayer of the Church, so that attuning our minds to our voices' *(Rule of St Benedict)* e may give fitting praise and worship to God.

Alan Rees OSB

Contents

Foreword	3
Celebration of Evening Prayer	4
First and Third Sundays of Advent	5
Second and Fourth Sundays of Advent	9
Christmastide	14
Lent	20
Palm Sunday	27
Eastertide	33
Pentecost	39
Holy Trinity	44
Corpus Christi	49
Sundays in Ordinary Time	
Psalter Week 1	54
Psalter Week 2	59
Psalter Week 3	64
Psalter Week 4	69
The Blessed Virgin Mary	74
The Lord's Prayer	80
Antiphons of Our Lady	82
Common texts for the Introduction, Canticle and Dismissal	90
Psalms which may be used instead of Psalm 109	93
Suggested hymns	96

Celebration of Evening Prayer

The following Ministers are required for the celebration of Evening Prayer:

Presider or Leader (priest, deacon, lay person)
Reader (for Scripture reading and Intercessions)
Cantor or cantors
Organist

If a priest or deacon presides, he may wear a cope and stole, and incense may be offered at the singing of the Magnificat.

The Office begins with the **Introduction** on page 90 followed by a **Hymn**. A list of suggested hymns is given on page 96. Other hymns may be used provided they fit in with the theme of the Sunday or the solemnity being celebrated. Hymns of the 'chorus' type should be avoided in the Divine Office.

Psalmody

The psalmody of Vespers consists of two psalms, well suited to the Hour and to celebration with the people, followed by a canticle from the Epistle or Revelation. (GILH ¶43)

As Psalm 109 appears every Sunday and solemnity, alternative psalms are suggested on pages 93-95, in accordance with GILH ¶246/7.

The antiphon should be sung by the Cantor and repeated by All. At the end of the psalm, it can be sung by everyone together. The Cantor sings the psalm alternately with the People. Antiphons and psalms should be sung lightly and in a flowing manner, giving due emphasis to word accents.

In the single and simple method of pointing the psalms used in this volume, the move to the note after the reciting note is marked by the underlining of the syllable. So,

1. When Israel came <u>forth</u> from Egypt,
   Jacob's family from an <u>a</u>lien people,
   Judah became <u>the</u> Lord's temple,
   Israel be<u>came</u> God's kingdom.

When Israel came forth from Egypt,   Jacob's family from an a – lien people,

Judah became the Lord's temple,   Israel be – came God's kingdom.

The principle of this system, championed by the late Dom Gregory Murray, is that the change of note corresponds with the second syllable before the final stressed syllable of the line. This may sound complicated but accords fairly closely with how the line would be spoken in ordinary speech.

Very occasionally a psalm will have strophes that not of equal length. Where this occurs, the psalm to is printed with a bracket over that portion of psalm tone to be omitted in the shorter strophe.

Canticle

The antiphon given for each Sunday should be sung the Cantor and repeated by All. The Canticle (see p. 91 for those days without a proper text) follows and the end the antiphon is again sung by everybody.

Scripture Reading

A short reading is given in this book. However longer scripture reading may be chosen in accordar with GILH ¶46. A brief homily may follow and/o silent pause for reflection.

Responsory

In response to the Word of God, there may be responsorial song or short responsory. The Can should sing the Response which is repeated by A The People repeat the Response after each of the inv cations sung by the Cantor.

The Responsory may be omitted if desired (GILH ¶4

Magnificat

The Canticle *Magnificat,* the Song of Mary, express praise and thanksgiving for our redemption and h been in popular use for centuries in the Roman Churc The Antiphon varies according to the Sunday or Fea A choice of antiphons is given for the Ordina Sundays of the Year.

To simplify use and to enable melodies to become fa iliar, only a limited number of texts from the Divi Office have been used in this edition, in accordan with GILH ¶246/7.

The Magnificat should be sung in the same way as t Psalms.

Intercessions, The Lord's Prayer, Concluding Praye Dismissal

Intercessions are provided for feasts and seasons, togeth with sung responses. However, other prayers may l taken from the Divine Office or other suitable sources.

Our Father may be said or sung. Two settings are pr vided on pages 80 and 81, but other familiar settin may be used.

The concluding prayer is said by the Presider and t blessing and dismissal is given according to GILH ¶54

Evening Prayer may conclude with one of the antipho of Our Lady which are found on page 82ff.

First and Third Sundays of Advent

Introduction
Page 90

Hymn
Page 96

Psalm 109

Re - joice great - ly, O daugh-ter of Si - on, shout with glad - ness,

daugh - ter of Je - ru - sa - lem, al - le - lu - ia.

* Omit in verses 5 and 6

1. The Lord's revelation to my Master:
   'Sit on my right;
   your foes I will put beneath your feet.'

2. The Lord will wield from Zion
   your sceptre of power;
   rule in the midst of all your foes.

3. A prince from the day of your birth
   on the holy mountains;
   from the womb before the dawn I begot you.

4. The Lord has sworn an oath and will not change.
   'You are a priest for ever,
   a priest like Melchizedek of old.'

5. The Master standing at your right hand
   will shatter rulers in the day of wrath,

6. He shall drink from the stream by the wayside,
   will stand with head held high.

7. Glory be to the Father and to the Son
   and to the Holy Spirit.
   As it was in the beginning, is now
   and ever shall be.
   World without end. Amen.

Psalm 113a

Be-hold, the Lord will come on the clouds of heav'n with great strength, al-le-lu - ia.

1. When Israel came <u>forth</u> from Egypt,
Jacob's family from an <u>a</u>lien people,
Judah became <u>the</u> Lord's temple,
Israel be<u>came</u> God's kingdom.

2. The sea fled <u>at</u> the sight,
the Jordan turned back <u>on</u> its course,
the mountains <u>leapt</u> like rams
and the hills like <u>year</u>ling sheep.

3. Why was it, sea, <u>that</u> you fled,
that you turned back, Jordan, <u>on</u> your course?

Mountains, that you <u>leapt</u> like rams;
hills, like <u>year</u>ling sheep?

4. Tremble, O earth, be<u>fore</u> the Lord,
in the presence of the <u>God</u> of Jacob,
who turns the rock in<u>to</u> a pool
and flint into a <u>spring</u> of water.

5. Glory be to the Father and to the Son
and to the <u>Ho</u>ly Spirit.
As it was in the beginning, is now
and <u>ev</u>er shall be.
World without <u>end</u>. Amen.

Canticle (Revelation 19:1-2, 5-7)

Great will be his reign   and peace will be e - ver - last - ing, al - le - lu - ia.

See page 91 for the Canticle

Reading: Philippians 4:4, 7

Rejoice in the Lord always; again I will say, rejoice. Let your gentleness be known to everyone. The Lord is near. Do not worry about anything, but in everything by prayer and supplication with thanksgiving let your requests be made known to God. And the peace of God, which surpasses all understanding, will guard your hearts and your minds in Christ Jesus.

Responsory

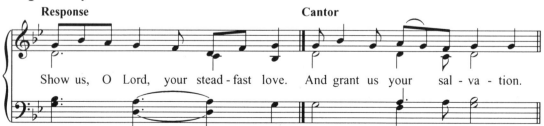

Response

Cantor

Show us, O Lord, your stead - fast love. And grant us your sal - va - tion.

Cantor

Give praise to the Fa - ther, the Son and Ho - ly Spi - rit.

Magnificat

Ma - ry, do not be a - fraid, for you have found fa - vour with God. Be -

hold, you will con - ceive and bear a son, al - le - lu - ia.

* Omit in verse 4

1. My soul glorifies the Lord,
   my spirit rejoices in God, my Saviour.
   He looks on his servant in her lowliness;
   henceforth all ages will call me blessed.

2. The Almighty works marvels for me.
   Holy his name!
   His mercy is from age to age,
   on those who fear him.

3. He puts forth his arm in strength
   and scatters the proud-hearted.
   He casts the mighty from their thrones
   and raises the lowly.

4. He fills the starving with good things,
   sends the rich away empty.

5. He protects Israel, his servant,
   remembering his mercy,
   the mercy promised to our fathers,
   to Abraham and his sons for ever.

6. Glory be to the Father and to the Son
   and to the Holy Spirit.
   As it was in the beginning, is now
   and ever shall be.
   World without end. Amen.

Intercessions

Leader In peace let us pray to the Lord.
Lord, bring us wisdom, fresh understanding
and new vision.

All *(sung after each Intercession)*

Come, Lord, do not de - lay.

Leader Lord, bring comfort to those in pain,
reassurance to the fearful,
peace of mind to the anxious.

Leader Lord Jesus, heal our misunderstandings
and help us to show genuine love
for each other.

Leader Let us pray to our heavenly Father
in the words the Lord Jesus gave us.

All Our Father *(pages 80-81)*

Concluding Prayer

Sunday 1
Grant, almighty Father,
that when Christ comes again we may go out to meet him,
bearing the harvest of good works achieved by your grace.
We pray that he will receive us into the company of the saints
and call us into the kingdom of heaven.
(We make our prayer) through our Lord.

Sunday 3
Grant, almighty God, that looking forward in faith
to the feast of our Lord's birth,
we may feel all the happiness our Saviour brings,
and celebrate his coming with unfailing joy.
(We make our prayer) through our Lord.

Blessing
Page 92

This Office may conclude with an antiphon of Our Lady (page 82ff)

Second and Fourth Sundays of Advent

Introduction
Page 90

Hymn
Page 96

Psalm 109

Re - joice great - ly, O daugh-ter of Si - on, shout with glad - ness,

daugh - ter of Je - ru - sa - lem, al - le - lu - ia.

* Omit in verses 5 and 6

1. The Lord's revelation <u>to</u> my Master:
   'Sit <u>on</u> my right;
   your foes I will put be<u>neath</u> your feet.'

2. The Lord will <u>wield</u> from Zion
   your scep<u>tre</u> of power;
   rule in the midst of <u>all</u> your foes.

3. A prince from the day <u>of</u> your birth
   on the <u>holy</u> mountains;
   from the womb before the dawn <u>I</u> begot you.

4. The Lord has sworn an oath and <u>will</u> not change.
   'You are a <u>priest</u> for ever,
   a priest like Melchize<u>dek</u> of old.'

5. The Master standing <u>at</u> your right hand
   will shatter rulers in the <u>day</u> of wrath,

6. He shall drink from the stream <u>by</u> the wayside,
   will stand with <u>head</u> held high.

7. Glory be to the Father and to the Son
   and to the <u>Holy</u> Spirit.
   As it was in the beginning, is now
   and <u>ever</u> shall be.
   World without <u>end</u>. Amen.

Psalm 113

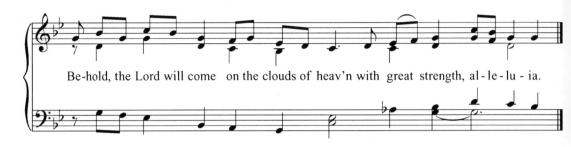

Be-hold, the Lord will come on the clouds of heav'n with great strength, al - le - lu - ia.

1. Not to us, Lord, not to us,
   but to your name give the glory
   for the sake of your love and your truth,
   lest the heathen say: 'Where is their God?'

2. But our God is in the heavens;
   whatever God wills, God does.
   Their idols are silver and gold,
   the work of human hands.

3. They have mouths but they cannot speak;
   they have eyes but they cannot see;
   they have ears but they cannot hear;
   they have nostrils but they cannot smell.

4. With their hands they cannot feel;
      with their feet they cannot walk.
   (No sound comes from their throats.)
   Their makers will come to be like them
   and so will all who trust in them.

5. Israel's family, trust in the Lord;
   he is your help and your shield.
   Aaron's family, trust in the Lord;
   he is your help and your shield.

6. You who fear the Lord, trust in the Lord;
   he is your help and your shield.
   The Lord remembers and will bless us;
   will bless the family of Israel.
      (will bless the family of Aaron.)

7. The Lord will bless those who fear him,
   the little no less than the great;
   to you may the Lord grant increase,
   to you and all your children.

8. May you be blessed by the Lord,
   the maker of heaven and earth.
   The heavens belong to the Lord
   but to us God has given the earth.

9. The dead shall not praise the Lord,
   nor those who go down into the silence.
   But we who live bless the Lord
   now and for ever. Amen.

10. Glory be to the Father and to the Son
      and to the Holy Spirit.
    As it was in the beginning, is now
      and ever shall be.
    World Without end. Amen.

Canticle (Revelation 19:1-2, 5-7)

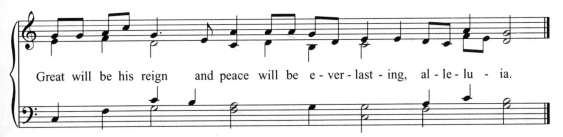

Great will be his reign and peace will be e-ver-last-ing, al-le-lu - ia.

See page 91 for the Canticle

Reading: Philippians 4:4, 7

Rejoice in the Lord always; again I will say, rejoice. Let your gentleness be known to everyone. The Lord is near. Do not worry about anything, but in everything by prayer and supplication with thanksgiving let your requests be made known to God. And the peace of God, which surpasses all understanding, will guard your hearts and your minds in Christ Jesus.

Responsory

Response   **Cantor**

Show us, O Lord, your stead-fast love. And grant us your sal - va - tion.

Cantor

Give praise to the Fa - ther, the Son and Ho - ly Spi - rit.

Magnificat

Bles-sed are you, O Ma - ry, for you have be - lieved. The Lord's

pro - mise to you will be ful - filled. Al - le - lu - ia.

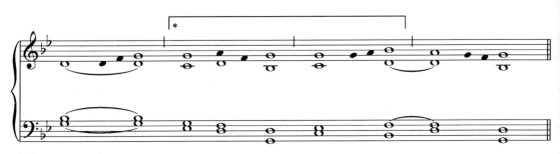

* *Omit in verse 4*

1. My soul glorifies the Lord,
   my spirit rejoices in God, my Saviour.
   He looks on his servant in her lowliness;
   henceforth all ages will call me blessed.

2. The Almighty works marvels for me.
   Holy his name!
   His mercy is from age to age,
   on those who fear him.

3. He puts forth his arm in strength
   and scatters the proud-hearted.
   He casts the mighty from their thrones
   and raises the lowly.

4. He fills the starving with good things,
   sends the rich away empty.

5. He protects Israel, his servant,
   remembering his mercy,
   the mercy promised to our fathers,
   to Abraham and his sons for ever.

6. Glory be to the Father and to the Son
   and to the Holy Spirit.
   As it was in the beginning, is now
   and ever shall be.
   World without end. Amen.

Intercessions

Leader   In peace let us pray to the Lord.
Lord, where we are blind to your presence
give us sight.

All *(sung after each Intercession)*

Come,   Lord,   do   not de - lay.

Leader   Lord, help people and nations
to grow in mutual respect,
and bring healing where
communication has broken down.

Leader   Lord Jesus, born of Mary,
come anew into our world.

Leader   Let us pray to our heavenly Father
in the words the Lord Jesus gave us.

All   Our Father *(pages 80-81)*

Concluding Prayer

Sunday 2
Almighty and merciful God,
let neither our daily work nor the cares of this life
prevent us from hastening to meet your Son.
Enlighten us with your wisdom and lead us into his company.
(We make our prayer) through our Lord.

Sunday 4
Lord, open our hearts to your grace.
Through the angel's message to Mary we have learned to believe
in the incarnation of Christ your Son.
Lead us by his passion and cross to the glory of his resurrection.
(We make our prayer) through our Lord.

Blessing
Page 92

The Office may conclude with an antiphon of Our Lady (page 82ff)

Christmastide

Introduction
Page 90

Hymn
Page 96

Psalm 109

A new day of re-demp-tion has dawned for us. It was pre-pared from of old and holds the pro-mise of e-ter-nal joy.

* Omit in verses 5 and 6

1. The Lord's revelation <u>to</u> my Master:
   'Sit <u>on</u> my right;
   your foes I will put be<u>neath</u> your feet.'

2. The Lord will <u>wield</u> from Zion
   your scep<u>tre</u> of power;
   rule in the midst of <u>all</u> your foes.

3. A prince from the day <u>of</u> your birth
   on the <u>ho</u>ly mountains;
   from the womb before the dawn <u>I</u> begot you.

4. The Lord has sworn an oath and <u>will</u> not change.
   'You are a <u>priest</u> for ever,
   a priest like Melchize<u>dek</u> of old.'

5. The Master standing <u>at</u> your right hand
   will shatter rulers in the <u>day</u> of wrath,

6. He shall drink from the stream <u>by</u> the wayside
   will stand with <u>head</u> held high.

7. Glory be to the Father and to the Son
   and to the <u>Ho</u>ly Spirit.
   As it was in the beginning, is now
   and <u>ev</u>er shall be.
   World without <u>end</u>. Amen.

The word was God in the be-gin-ning and be-fore all times;

now he is born for us, the Sa-viour of the world.

1. Not to us, Lord, not to us,
   but to your name give the glory
   for the sake of your love and your truth,
   lest the heathen say: 'Where is their God?'

2. But our God is in the heavens;
   whatever God wills, God does.
   Their idols are silver and gold,
   the work of human hands.

3. They have mouths but they cannot speak;
   they have eyes but they cannot see;
   they have ears but they cannot hear;
   they have nostrils but they cannot smell.

4. With their hands they cannot feel;
   with their feet they cannot walk.
   (No sound comes from their throats.)
   Their makers will come to be like them
   and so will all who trust in them.

5. Israel's family, trust in the Lord;
   he is your help and your shield.
   Aaron's family, trust in the Lord;
   he is your help and your shield.

6. You who fear the Lord, trust in the Lord;
   he is your help and your shield.
   The Lord remembers and will bless us;
   will bless the family of Israel.
        (will bless the family of Aaron.)

7. The Lord will bless those who fear him,
   the little no less than the great;
   to you may the Lord grant increase,
   to you and all your children.

8. May you be blessed by the Lord,
   the maker of heaven and earth.
   The heavens belong to the Lord
   but to us God has given the earth.

9. The dead shall not praise the Lord,
   nor those who go down into the silence.
   But we who live bless the Lord
   now and for ever. Amen.

10. Glory be to the Father and to the Son
        and to the Holy Spirit.
    As it was in the beginning, is now
        and ever shall be.
    World without end. Amen.

Canticle (Colossians 1:12-20)

The Lord, the King of kings, has been born for us on earth: the sal - va - tion of the world, our re-demp-tion, has come to us, al - le - lu - ia.

* Omit in verse 1

1. Let us give thanks to the Father,
   who has qualified us to share
   in the inheritance of the saints in light.

2. He has delivered us from the
      dominion of darkness
   and transferred us to the kingdom
      of his beloved Son,
   in whom we have redemption,
   the forgiveness of sins.

3. He is the image of the invisible God,
   the firstborn of all creation,
   for in him all things were created,
      in heaven and on earth,
   visible and invisible.

4. All things were created
   through him and for him.
   He is before all things,
   and in him all things hold together.

5. He is the head of the body, the Church;
   he is the beginning,
   the firstborn from the dead,
   that in everything he might be pre-eminent.

6. For in him all the fulness of God
      was pleased to dwell,
   and through him to reconcile to
      himself all things,
   whether on earth or in heaven,
   making peace by the blood of his cross.

7. Glory be to the Father and to the Son
      and to the Holy Spirit.
   As it was in the beginning, is now
      and ever shall be.
   World without end. Amen.

Reading: 1 John 1:1-3

We declare to you what was from the beginning, what we have heard,
what we have seen with our eyes, what we have looked at and touched
with our hands, concerning the word of life – this life was revealed, and
we have seen it and testify to it, and declare to you the eternal life that
was with the Father and was revealed to us – we declare to you what we
have seen and heard so that you also may have fellowship with us; and
truly our fellowship is with the Father and with his Son Jesus Christ.

Responsory

Response

The Word be-came flesh, al - le - lu - ia, al - le - lu - ia.

Cantor

And lived a - mong us.

Cantor

Praise the Fa - ther, the Son and Ho - ly Spi - rit.

17

Magnificat

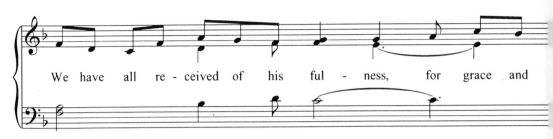

We have all re - ceived of his ful - ness, for grace and

truth have come through Je - sus Christ.

* Omit in verse 4

1. My soul glorifies the Lord,
   my spirit rejoices in God, my Saviour.
   He looks on his servant in her lowliness;
   henceforth all ages will call me blessed.

2. The Almighty works marvels for me.
   Holy his name!
   His mercy is from age to age,
   on those who fear him.

3. He puts forth his arm in strength
   and scatters the proud-hearted.
   He casts the mighty from their thrones
   and raises the lowly.

4. He fills the starving with good things,
   sends the rich away empty.

5. He protects Israel, his servant,
   remembering his mercy,
   the mercy promised to our fathers,
   to Abraham and his sons for ever.

6. Glory be to the Father and to the Son
   and to the Holy Spirit.
   As it was in the beginning, is now
   and ever shall be.
   World without end. Amen.

Intercessions

Christmas

Leader   In peace let us pray to the Lord.
May the Light of Christ pierce the darkness of our world
at this Christmastide and fill all people with hope.

All *(sung after each Intercession)*

Light of the world, shine in our dark-ness.

Leader   May the compassion of Christ touch all those
who need comfort, help and healing at this time.

Leader   May the love of Christ enfold our families,
and all who are homeless or lonely;
may we learn to value one another more.

Leader   Let us pray to our heavenly Father
in the words the Lord Jesus gave us.

All   Our Father (page 80-81)

Epiphany

Leader   In peace let us pray to the Lord.
We pray that the Church throughout the world may
always be ready to follow the way of the Lord.

All   *(see above for response)*

Leader   We pray for those who have lost their way,
and for all who are finding their journey through life
lonely or frightening.

Leader   We pray for those who have come to the end of their
earthly journey and are soon to meet Christ.

Leader   Let us pray to our heavenly Father
in the words the Lord Jesus gave us.

All   Our Father *(page 80-81)*

Concluding Prayer

Almighty, ever-living God, light of every faithful soul,
fill the world with your glory,
and reveal to all nations the splendour of your presence.
(We make our prayer) through our Lord.

Blessing
Page 92

The Office may conclude with an antiphon of Our Lady (page 82ff)

Lent

Introduction
Page 90

Hymn
Page 96

Psalm 109

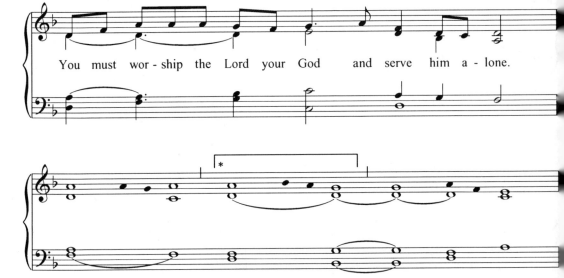

You must wor - ship the Lord your God and serve him a - lone.

* Omit in verses 5 and 6

1. The Lord's revelation <u>to</u> my Master:
   'Sit <u>on</u> my right;
   your foes I will put be<u>neath</u> your feet.'

2. The Lord will <u>wield</u> from Zion
   your scep<u>tre</u> of power;
   rule in the midst of <u>all</u> your foes.

3. A prince from the day <u>of</u> your birth
   on the <u>holy</u> mountains;
   from the womb before the dawn <u>I</u> begot you.

4. The Lord has sworn an oath and <u>will</u> not change.
   'You are a <u>priest</u> for ever,
   a priest like Melchize<u>dek</u> of old.'

5. The Master standing <u>at</u> your right hand
   will shatter rulers in the <u>day</u> of wrath,

6. He shall drink from the stream <u>by</u> the wayside
   will stand with <u>head</u> held high.

7. Glory be to the Father and to the Son
   and to the <u>Holy</u> Spirit.
   As it was in the beginning, is now
   and <u>ever</u> shall be.
   World without <u>end</u>. Amen.

Now is the fa-vour-a-ble time: this is the day of sal-va-tion.

1. When Israel came <u>forth</u> from Egypt,
   Jacob's family from an <u>a</u>lien people,
   Judah became <u>the</u> Lord's temple,
   Israel be<u>came</u> God's kingdom.

2. The sea fled <u>at</u> the sight,
   the Jordan turned back <u>on</u> its course,
   the mountains <u>leapt</u> like rams
   and the hills like <u>year</u>ling sheep.

3. Why was it, sea, <u>that</u> you fled,
   that you turned back, Jordan, <u>on</u> your course?
   Mountains, that you <u>leapt</u> like rams;
   hills, like <u>year</u>ling sheep?

4. Tremble, O earth, be<u>fore</u> the Lord,
   in the presence of the <u>God</u> of Jacob,
   who turns the rock in<u>to</u> a pool
   and flint into a <u>spring</u> of water.

5. Glory be to the Father and to the Son
   and to the <u>Ho</u>ly Spirit.
   As it was in the beginning, is now
   and <u>ev</u>er shall be.
   World without <u>end</u>. Amen.

Canticle

Ours were the suf-fer-ings he bore, ours the sor-rows he car-ried.

Omit in verse 1

1. Christ suffered for you,
   leaving you an example
   that you should follow in his steps.

2. He committed no sin;
   no guile was found on his lips.
   When he was reviled,
   he did not revile in return.

3. When he suffered,
   he did not threaten;
   but he trusted to him
   who judges justly.

4. He himself bore our sins
   in his body on the tree,
   that we might die to sin
   and live to righteousness.
   By his wounds you have been healed.

5. Glory be to the Father and to the Son
   and to the Holy Spirit.
   As it was in the beginning, is now
   and ever shall be.
   World without end. Amen.

Reading: 1 Corinthians 9:24-27

Do you not know that in a race the runners all compete, but only one receives the prize? Run in such a way that you may win it. Athletes exercise self-control in all things; they do it to receive a perishable wreath, but we an imperishable one. So I do not run aimlessly, nor do I box as though beating the air; but I punish my body and enslave it, so that after proclaiming to others I myself should not be disqualified.

Responsory

Response

Hear us, Lord, and have mer - cy, for we have sinned a - gainst you.

Cantor

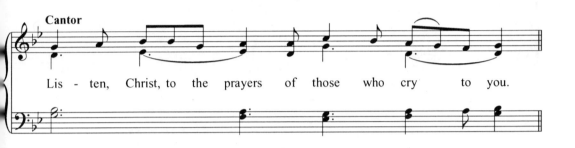

Lis - ten, Christ, to the prayers of those who cry to you.

Cantor

Give praise to the Fa - ther and Son and to the Ho - ly Spi - rit.

Magnificat

Keep watch o-ver us, e-ter-nal Sa-viour. Let us not be o-ver-come by e-vil for you are our Help-er at all times.

* Omit in verse 4

1. My soul glorifies the Lord,
   my spirit rejoices in God, my Saviour.
   He looks on his servant in her lowliness;
   henceforth all ages will call me blessed.

2. The Almighty works marvels for me.
   Holy his name!
   His mercy is from age to age,
   on those who fear him.

3. He puts forth his arm in strength
   and scatters the proud-hearted.
   He casts the mighty from their thrones
   and raises the lowly.

4. He fills the starving with good things,
   sends the rich away empty.

5. He protects Israel, his servant,
   remembering his mercy,
   the mercy promised to our fathers,
   to Abraham and his sons for ever.

6. Glory be to the Father and to the Son
   and to the Holy Spirit.
   As it was in the beginning, is now
   and ever shall be.
   World without end. Amen.

Intercessions

Sundays 1, 3 and 5

Leader In peace let us pray to the Lord.
Lord, we pray for our damaged world
with all its weakness and longings,
its potential and hope.

All *(sung after each Intercession)*

Lord, give life to your peo - ple.

Leader Lord, you are gentle and humble in heart;
grant us a share in your spirit of compassion
and your patient endurance.

Leader Let us work with you to fill the world with your spirit;
may our earthly city grow in justice, love and peace.

Leader Let us pray to our heavenly Father
in the words the Lord Jesus gave us.

All Our Father *(pages 80-81)*

Sundays 2 and 4

Leader In peace let us pray to the Lord.
Lord, may we open our lives to others,
share their laughter and tears, and grow in love.

All *(see above for response)*

Leader Let your peace spread to the ends of the earth;
may the signs of your presence be visible everywhere.

Leader Lord, set us free from all evil;
in the confusion of our lives
show us the things that really matter.

Leader Let us pray to our heavenly Father
in the words the Lord Jesus gave us.

All Our Father *(pages 80-81)*

Concluding Prayer

Sunday 1
Through our annual Lenten observance, Lord,
deepen our understanding of the mystery of Christ,
and make it a reality in the conduct of our lives.
(We make our prayer) through our Lord.

Sunday 2
God our Father, you bid us listen to your Son,
the well-beloved. Nourish our hearts on your word,
purify the eyes of our mind, and fill us with joy
at the vision of your glory.
(We make our prayer) through our Lord.

Sunday 3
God our Father, in your infinite love and goodness
you have shown us that prayer, fasting, and almsgiving
are remedies for sin: accept the humble admission of
our guilt, and when our conscience weighs us down
let your unfailing mercy raise us up.
(We make our prayer) through our Lord.

Sunday 4
Lord God, in your surpassing wisdom you reconcile us
to yourself through your Word. Grant that your Christian
people may come with eager faith and ready will to
celebrate the Easter festival.
(We make our prayer) through our Lord.

Sunday 5
Lord our God, your Son so loved the world that he gave
himself up to death for our sake. Strengthen us by your
grace, and give us a heart willing to live by that same love.
(We make our prayer) through our Lord.

Blessing
Page 92

The Office may conclude with an antiphon of Our Lady (page 82ff)

Palm Sunday

Introduction
Page 90

Hymn
Page 96

Psalm 109

He was wound-ed and hum-bled, but God has raised him up with his own right hand.

*Omit in verses 5 and 6

1. The Lord's revelation <u>to</u> my Master:
   'Sit <u>on</u> my right;
   your foes I will put be<u>neath</u> your feet.'

2. The Lord will <u>wield</u> from Zion
   your scep<u>tre</u> of power;
   rule in the midst of <u>all</u> your foes.

3. A prince from the day <u>of</u> your birth
   on the <u>ho</u>ly mountains;
   from the womb before the dawn <u>I</u> begot you.

4. The Lord has sworn an oath and <u>will</u> not change.
   'You are a <u>priest</u> for ever,
   a priest like Melchize<u>dek</u> of old.'

5. The Master standing <u>at</u> your right hand
   will shatter rulers in the <u>day</u> of wrath,

6. He shall drink from the stream <u>by</u> the wayside,
   will stand with <u>head</u> held high.

7. Glory be to the Father and to the Son
   and to the <u>Ho</u>ly Spirit.
   As it was in the beginning, is now
   and <u>ev</u>er shall be.
   World without <u>end</u>. Amen.

Psalm 113b

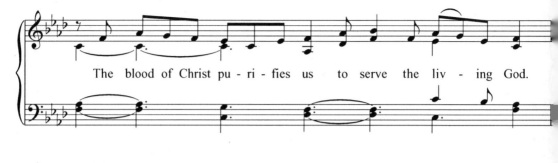

The blood of Christ pu - ri - fies us to serve the liv - ing God.

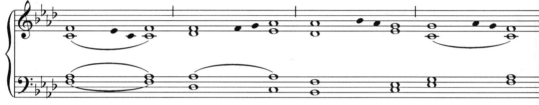

1. Not to us, Lord, <u>not</u> to us,
   but to your name <u>give</u> the glory
   for the sake of your love <u>and</u> your truth,
   lest the heathen say: 'Where <u>is</u> their God?'

2. But our God is <u>in</u> the heavens;
   whatever God <u>wills</u>, God does.
   Their idols are sil<u>ver</u> and gold,
   the work of <u>human</u> hands.

3. They have mouths but they <u>cannot</u> speak;
   they have eyes but they <u>cannot</u> see;
   they have ears but they <u>cannot</u> hear;
   they have nostrils but they <u>cannot</u> smell.

4. With their hands they cannot feel;
   with their feet they <u>cannot</u> walk.
   (No sound comes <u>from</u> their throats.)
   Their makers will come to <u>be</u> like them
   and so will all who <u>trust</u> in them.

5. Israel's family, trust <u>in</u> the Lord;
   he is your help <u>and</u> your shield.
   Aaron's family, trust <u>in</u> the Lord;
   he is your help <u>and</u> your shield.

6. You who fear the Lord, trust <u>in</u> the Lord;
   he is your help <u>and</u> your shield.
   The Lord remembers <u>and</u> will bless us;
   will bless the family of Israel.
      (will bless the fami<u>ly</u> of Aaron.)

7. The Lord will bless <u>those</u> who fear him,
   the little no less <u>than</u> the great;
   to you may the <u>Lord</u> grant increase,
   to you and <u>all</u> your children.

8. May you be blessed <u>by</u> the Lord,
   the maker of hea<u>ven</u> and earth.
   The heavens belong <u>to</u> the Lord
   but to us God has <u>given</u> the earth.

9. The dead shall not <u>praise</u> the Lord,
   nor those who go down <u>into</u> the silence.
   But we who live <u>bless</u> the Lord
   now and for <u>ever</u>. Amen.

10. Glory be to the Father and to the Son
       and to the <u>Holy</u> Spirit.
    As it was in the beginning, is now
       and <u>ever</u> shall be.
    World without <u>end</u>. Amen.

Canticle

Ours were the suf-fer-ings he bore, ours the sor-rows he car-ried.

* Omit in verse 1

1. Christ suffered for you,
   leaving you an example
   that you should follow in his steps.

2. He committed no sin;
   no guile was found on his lips.
   When he was reviled,
   he did not revile in return.

3. When he suffered,
   he did not threaten;
   but he trusted to him
   who judges justly.

4. He himself bore our sins
   in his body on the tree,
   that we might die to sin
   and live to righteousness.
   By his wounds you have been healed.

5. Glory be to the Father and to the Son
   and to the Holy Spirit.
   As it was in the beginning, is now
   and ever shall be.
   World without end. Amen.

Reading: Acts 13: 26-30a

My brothers, you descendants of Abraham's family, and others who fear God, to us the message of this salvation has been sent. Because the residents of Jerusalem and their leaders did not recognize him or understand the words of the prophets that are read every sabbath, they fulfilled those words by condemning him. Even though they found no cause for a sentence of death, they asked Pilate to have him killed. When they had carried out everything that was written about him, they took him down from the tree and laid him in a tomb. But God raised him from the dead.

Responsory

Response

We wor - ship you, Christ, and we bless you.

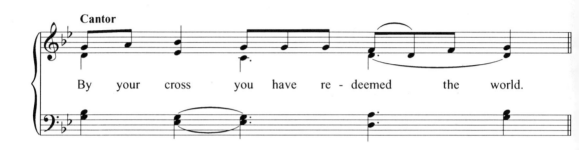

Cantor

By your cross you have re - deemed the world.

Cantor

Praise the Fa - ther, the Son and Ho - ly Spi - rit.

Magnificat

When I am lift-ed up from the earth I shall draw all peo-ple to my-self.

Omit in verse 4

1. My soul glorifies the Lord,
   my spirit rejoices in God, my Saviour.
   He looks on his servant in her lowliness;
   henceforth all ages will call me blessed.

2. The Almighty works marvels for me.
   Holy his name!
   His mercy is from age to age,
   on those who fear him.

3. He puts forth his arm in strength
   and scatters the proud-hearted.
   He casts the mighty from their thrones
   and raises the lowly.

4. He fills the starving with good things,
   sends the rich away empty.

5. He protects Israel, his servant,
   remembering his mercy,
   the mercy promised to our fathers,
   to Abraham and his sons for ever.

6. Glory be to the Father and to the Son
     and to the Holy Spirit.
   As it was in the beginning, is now
     and ever shall be.
   World without end. Amen.

Intercessions

Leader   In peace let us pray to the Lord.
Lord, we pray for all who suffer from others' sin;
may your heavenly love mend their broken lives.

All *(sung after each Intercession)*

Lord,   give life   to your peo - ple.

Leader   Lord, teach us to be united with your passion
in times of trouble and distress;
may your saving power shine forth in our lives.

Leader   Lord, you humbled yourself even to accepting
death on a cross; give us a share in your
obedience and patience.

Leader   Let us pray to our heavenly Father
in the words the Lord Jesus gave us.

All   Our Father *(pages 80-81)*

Concluding Prayer

Almighty, ever-living God,
you gave our Saviour the command
to become man and undergo the cross,
as an example of humility for all people to follow.
We have the lessons of his sufferings:
give us also the fellowship of his resurrection.
(We make our prayer) through our Lord.

Blessing
Page 92

The Office may conclude with an antiphon of Our Lady (page 82ff)

Eastertide

Introduction
Page 90

Hymn
Page 96

Psalm 109

The Lord is ris - en and sits at the right hand of God. Al - le - lu - ia.

* Omit in verses 5 and 6

1. The Lord's revelation <u>to</u> my Master:
   'Sit <u>on</u> my right;
   your foes I will put be<u>neath</u> your feet.'

2. The Lord will <u>wield</u> from Zion
   your scep<u>tre</u> of power;
   rule in the midst of <u>all</u> your foes.

3. A prince from the day <u>of</u> your birth
   on the <u>ho</u>ly mountains;
   from the womb before the dawn <u>I</u> begot you.

4. The Lord has sworn an oath and <u>will</u> not change.
   'You are a <u>priest</u> for ever,
   a priest like Melchize<u>dek</u> of old.'

5. The Master standing <u>at</u> your right hand
   will shatter rulers in the <u>day</u> of wrath,

6. He shall drink from the stream <u>by</u> the wayside,
   will stand with <u>head</u> held high.

7. Glory be to the Father and to the Son
   and to the <u>Ho</u>ly Spirit.
   As it was in the beginning, is now
   and <u>ev</u>er shall be.
   World without <u>end</u>. Amen.

Psalm 113a

The Lord has de - li - vered his peo - ple. Al - le - lu - ia.

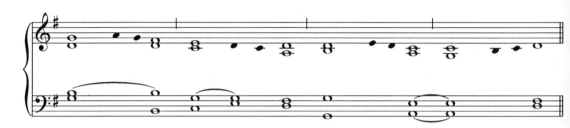

1. When Israel came <u>forth</u> from Egypt,
   Jacob's family from an <u>a</u>lien people,
   Judah became before <u>the</u> Lord's temple,
   Israel be<u>came</u> God's kingdom.

2. The sea fled <u>at</u> the sight,
   the Jordan turned back <u>on</u> its course,
   the mountains <u>leapt</u> like rams
   and the hills like <u>yearling</u> sheep.

3. Why was it, sea, <u>that</u> you fled,
   that you turned back, Jordan, <u>on</u> your course?
   Mountains, that you <u>leapt</u> like rams;
   hills, like <u>yearling</u> sheep?

4. Tremble, O earth, be<u>fore</u> the Lord,
   in the presence of the <u>God</u> of Jacob,
   who turns the rock in<u>to</u> a pool
   and flint into a <u>spring</u> of water.

5. Glory be to the Father and to the Son
     and to the <u>Ho</u>ly Spirit.
   As it was in the beginning, is now
     and <u>ever</u> shall be.
   World without <u>end</u>. Amen.

Canticle

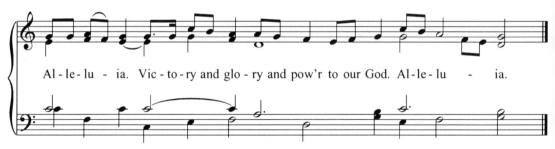

Al - le - lu - ia. Vic - to - ry and glo - ry and pow'r to our God. Al - le - lu - ia.

See page 91 for the Canticle

Reading: Hebrews 10:12-14

When Christ had offered for all time a single sacrifice for sins, 'he sat down at the right hand of God,' and since then has been waiting 'until his enemies would be made a footstool for his feet.' For by a single offering he has perfected for all time those who are sanctified.

Responsory

Response

The Lord has tru - ly ris'n. Al - le - lu - ia, al - le - lu - ia.

Cantor

He has ap - peared to Si - mon.

Cantor

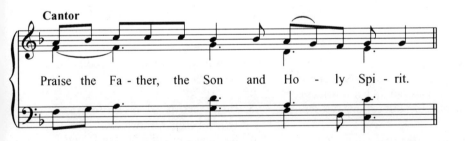

Praise the Fa - ther, the Son and Ho - ly Spi - rit.

Magnificat

During Eastertide (before the Ascension)

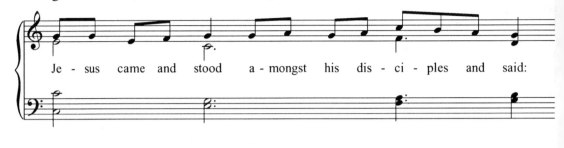

Je - sus came and stood a - mongst his dis - ci - ples and said:

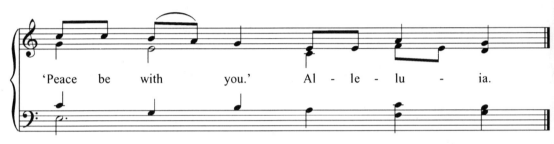

'Peace be with you.' Al - le - lu - ia.

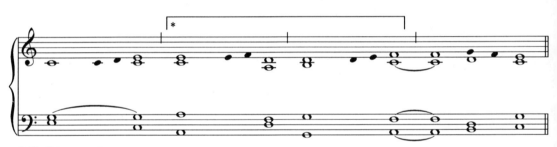

* Omit in verse 4

1. My soul glorifies the Lord,
   my spirit rejoices in God, my Saviour.
   He looks on his servant in her lowliness;
   henceforth all ages will call me blessed.

2. The Almighty works marvels for me.
   Holy his name!
   His mercy is from age to age,
   on those who fear him.

3. He puts forth his arm in strength
   and scatters the proud-hearted.
   He casts the mighty from their thrones
   and raises the lowly.

4. He fills the starving with good things,
   sends the rich away empty.

5. He protects Israel, his servant,
   remembering his mercy,
   the mercy promised to our fathers,
   to Abraham and his sons for ever.

6. Glory be to the Father and to the Son
   and to the Holy Spirit.
   As it was in the beginning, is now
   and ever shall be.
   World without end. Amen.

For Ascension and the Seventh Sunday of Easter

I will send you the Ad-vo-cate, the Spi-rit of truth, who comes from the

Fa-ther. He will be my wit-ness. Al-le-lu-ia.

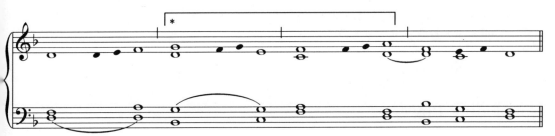

* Omit in verse 4

1. My soul glorifies the Lord,
   my spirit rejoices in <u>God</u>, my Saviour.
   He looks on his servant <u>in</u> her lowliness;
   henceforth all ages will <u>call</u> me blessed.

2. The Almighty works mar<u>vels</u> for me.
   Ho<u>ly</u> his name!
   His mercy is from <u>age</u> to age,
   on <u>those</u> who fear him.

3. He puts forth his <u>arm</u> in strength
   and scatters <u>the</u> proud-hearted.
   He casts the mighty <u>from</u> their thrones
   and rai<u>ses</u> the lowly.

4. He fills the starving <u>with</u> good things,
   sends the rich <u>away</u> empty.

5. He protects Isra<u>el</u>, his servant,
   remember<u>ing</u> his mercy,
   the mercy promised <u>to</u> our fathers,
   to Abraham and his <u>sons</u> for ever.

6. Glory be to the Father and to the Son
      and to the <u>Holy</u> Spirit.
   As it was in the beginning, is now
      and <u>ever</u> shall be.
   World without <u>end</u>. Amen.

Intercessions

Leader In peace let us pray to the Lord.
May the way which Jesus shows us
be the way we live out our daily lives.

All *(sung after each Intercession)*

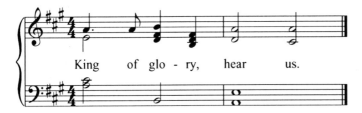

King of glo - ry, hear us.

Leader We pray for healing and wholeness in all who suffer;
may the risen Lord give them his transforming love.

Leader We pray to the Good Shepherd for all who have died
and for those who grieve for them; may he give his peace
to both the living and the dead.

Leader Let us pray to our heavenly Father
in the words the Lord Jesus gave us.

All   Our Father *(pages 80-81)*

Concluding Prayer

God of eternal compassion,
each Easter you rekindle the faith of your consecrated people.
Give them still greater grace,
so that all may truly understand
the waters in which they were cleansed,
the Spirit by which they were reborn,
the blood by which they were redeemed.
(We make our prayer) through our Lord.

Blessing

Cantor { Let us bless the Lord,
{ Go in the peace of Christ, } al - le - lu - ia, al - le - lu - ia.
All   Thanks be to God,

The Office may conclude with an antiphon of Our Lady (page 82ff)

Pentecost

Introduction
Page 90

Hymn
Page 96

Psalm 112

The Spi-rit of the Lord has filled the whole world, al - le - lu - ia.

Omit in verse 4

1. Praise, O servants of the Lord,
   praise the name of the Lord!
   May the name of the Lord be blessed
   both now and for evermore!
   From the rising of the sun to its setting
   praised be the name of the Lord!

2. High above all nations is the Lord,
   above the heavens God's glory.
   Who is like the Lord, our God,
   the one enthroned on high,
   who stoops from the heights to look down,
   to look down upon heaven and earth?

3. From the dust God lifts up the lowly,
   from the dungheap God raises the poor
   to set them in the company of rulers,
   yes, with the rulers of the people.
   To the childless wife God gives a home
   and gladdens her heart with children.

4. Glory be to the Father and to the Son
      and to the Holy Spirit.
   As it was in the beginning, is now
      and ever shall be.
   World without end. Amen.

Psalm 113a

Send forth your pow'r, Lord, from your ho - ly tem - ple in Je - ru - sa - lem, and bring to per - fec - tion your work a - mong us, al - le - lu - ia.

1. When Israel came forth from Egypt,
   Jacob's family from an alien people,
   Judah became before the Lord's temple,
   Israel became God's kingdom.

2. The sea fled at the sight,
   the Jordan turned back on its course,
   the mountains leapt like rams
   and the hills like yearling sheep.

3. Why was it, sea, that you fled,
   that you turned back, Jordan, on your course?
   Mountains, that you leapt like rams;
   hills, like yearling sheep?

4. Tremble, O earth, before the Lord,
   in the presence of the God of Jacob,
   who turns the rock into a pool
   and flint into a spring of water.

5. Glory be to the Father and to the Son
   and to the Holy Spirit.
   As it was in the beginning, is now
   and ever shall be.
   World without end. Amen.

Canticle

They were all filled with the Ho - ly Spi - rit and be-gan to speak. Al - le - lu - ia.

See page 91 for the Canticle

Reading: Ephesians 4:1-6

therefore, the prisoner in the Lord, beg you to lead a life worthy of the calling to which you have been called, with all humility and gentleness, with patience, bearing with one another in love, making every effort to maintain the unity of the Spirit in the bond of peace. There is one body and one Spirit, just as you were called to the one hope of your calling, one Lord, one faith, one baptism, one God and Father of all, who is above all and through all and in all.

Responsory

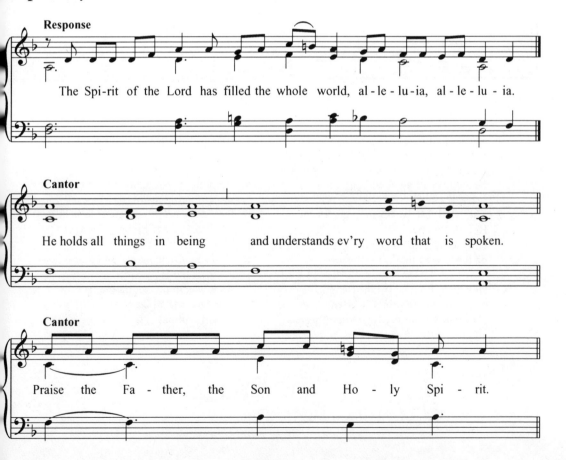

Response

The Spi-rit of the Lord has filled the whole world, al - le - lu - ia, al - le - lu - ia.

Cantor

He holds all things in being and understands ev'ry word that is spoken.

Cantor

Praise the Fa - ther, the Son and Ho - ly Spi - rit.

Magnificat

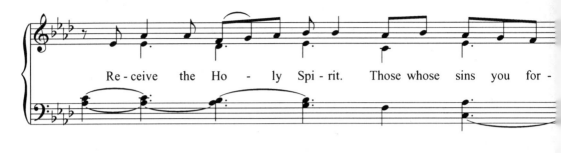

Re - ceive the Ho - ly Spi - rit. Those whose sins you for -

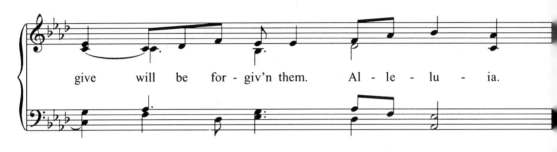

give will be for - giv'n them. Al - le - lu - ia.

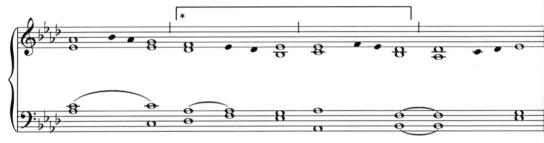

* Omit in verse 4

1. My soul glorifies the Lord,
   my spirit rejoices in God, my Saviour.
   He looks on his servant in her lowliness;
   henceforth all ages will call me blessed.

2. The Almighty works marvels for me.
   Holy his name!
   His mercy is from age to age,
   on those who fear him.

3. He puts forth his arm in strength
   and scatters the proud-hearted.
   He casts the mighty from their thrones
   and raises the lowly.

4. He fills the starving with good things,
   sends the rich away empty.

5. He protects Israel, his servant,
   remembering his mercy,
   the mercy promised to our fathers,
   to Abraham and his sons for ever.

6. Glory be to the Father and to the Son
   and to the Holy Spirit.
   As it was in the beginning, is now
   and ever shall be.
   World without end. Amen.

Intercessions

Leader In peace let us pray to the Lord.
We pray for Christians all over the world and for those
who doubt the truth; may our hearts be set ablaze
with love that we may walk as children of the light.

All *(sung after each Intercession)*

King of glo - ry, hear us.

Leader Lord, keep our eyes fixed on the new heaven
and new earth; make us care more deeply
and work more generously for our world and its future.

Leader Lord, you sent your disciples to proclaim the gospel
throughout the world; may all who spread your word
today be alive with your Holy Spirit.

Leader Let us pray to our heavenly Father
in the words the Lord Jesus gave us.

All Our Father *(pages 80-81)*

Concluding Prayer

Lord God,
you sanctify your Church in every race and nation
by the mystery we celebrate on this day.
Pour out the gifts of the Holy Spirit on all mankind,
and fulfil now in the hearts of your faithful
what you accomplished
when the Gospel was first preached on earth.
We make our prayer) through our Lord.

Blessing

Cantor { Let us bless the Lord,
Go in the peace of Christ, } al - le - lu - ia, al - le - lu - ia.
All Thanks be to God,

The Office may conclude with an antiphon of Our Lady (page 82ff)

43

Holy Trinity

Introduction
Page 90

Hymn
Page 96

Psalm 112

Give us free-dom, sal - va - tion and life, O bles - sed Tri - ni - ty.

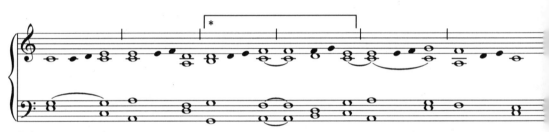

* Omit in verse 4

1. Praise, O servants of the Lord,
   praise the name of the Lord!
   May the name of the Lord be blessed
   both now and for evermore!
   From the rising of the sun to its setting
   praised be the name of the Lord!

2. High above all nations is the Lord,
   above the heavens God's glory.
   Who is like the Lord, our God,
   the one enthroned on high,
   who stoops from the heights to look down,
   to look down upon heaven and earth?

3. From the dust God lifts up the lowly,
   from the dungheap God raises the poor
   to set them in the company of rulers,
   yes, with the rulers of the people.
   To the childless wife God gives a home
   and gladdens her heart with children.

4. Glory be to the Father and to the Son
   and to the Holy Spirit.
   As it was in the beginning, is now
   and ever shall be.
   World without end. Amen.

O true, high-est and e - ver-last-ing Tri - ni - ty. Fa - ther, Son and Ho - ly Spi-rit.

1. When Israel came <u>forth</u> from Egypt,
   Jacob's family from an <u>a</u>lien people,
   Judah became <u>the</u> Lord's temple,
   Israel be<u>came</u> God's kingdom.

2. The sea fled <u>at</u> the sight,
   the Jordan turned back <u>on</u> its course,
   the mountains <u>leapt</u> like rams
   and the hills like <u>year</u>ling sheep.

3. Why was it, sea, <u>that</u> you fled,
   that you turned back, Jordan, <u>on</u> your course?
   Mountains, that you <u>leapt</u> like rams;
   hills, like <u>year</u>ling sheep?

4. Tremble, O earth, be<u>fore</u> the Lord,
   in the presence of the <u>God</u> of Jacob,
   who turns the rock in<u>to</u> a pool
   and flint into a <u>spring</u> of water.

5. Glory be to the Father and to the Son
   and to the <u>Holy</u> Spirit.
   As it was in the beginning, is now
   and <u>ever</u> shall be.
   World without <u>end</u>. Amen.

Canticle

Ho - ly, ho - ly, ho - ly is the Lord God al - migh - ty, who was, who is, and who is to come.

See page 91 for the Canticle

Reading: Ephesians 4:1-6

I therefore, the prisoner in the Lord, beg you to lead a life worthy of the calling to which you have been called, with all humility and gentleness, with patience, bearing with one another in love, making every effort to maintain the unity of the Spirit in the bond of peace. There is one body and one Spirit, just as you were called to the one hope of your calling, one Lord, one faith, one baptism, one God and Father of all, who is above all and through all and in all.

Responsory

Response

Let us bless the Fa - ther, and the Son and the Ho - ly Spi - rit.

Cantor

To God a - lone be all hon - our and glo - ry.

Cantor

Give praise to the Fa - ther, the Son and Ho - ly Spi - rit.

Magnificat

With our hearts and lips   we praise you, we wor - ship you and we bless you,

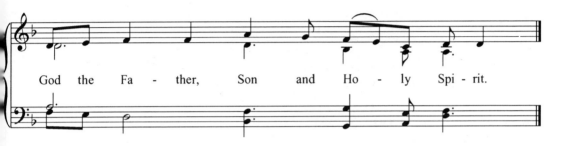

God   the   Fa - ther,   Son   and   Ho - ly   Spi - rit.

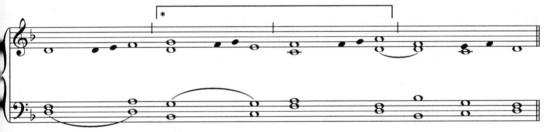

*Omit in verse 4

1. My soul glorifies the Lord,
   my spirit rejoices in God, my Saviour.
   He looks on his servant in her lowliness;
   henceforth all ages will call me blessed.

2. The Almighty works marvels for me.
   Holy his name!
   His mercy is from age to age,
   on those who fear him.

3. He puts forth his arm in strength
   and scatters the proud-hearted.
   He casts the mighty from their thrones
   and raises the lowly.

4. He fills the starving with good things,
   sends the rich away empty.

5. He protects Israel, his servant,
   remembering his mercy,
   the mercy promised to our fathers,
   to Abraham and his sons for ever.

6. Glory be to the Father and to the Son
   and to the Holy Spirit.
   As it was in the beginning, is now
   and ever shall be.
   World without end. Amen.

Intercessions

Leader   In peace let us pray to the Lord.
May the Church reflect the community and unity within the Trinity;
may there be love, mutual support and encouragement in the faith.

All *(sung after each Intercession)*

King   of glo - ry,   hear   us.

Leader   May there be love and respect in every household;
may there be thoughtfulness, consideration and trust.

Leader   May the world's leaders seek not personal power
but the public good; may all our communities
be built upon what is good, true, just and right.

Leader   Let us pray to our heavenly Father
in the words the Lord Jesus gave us.

All   Our Father *(pages 80-81)*

Concluding Prayer

God our Father,
you revealed the great mystery of your godhead to all people
when you sent into the world
the Word who is Truth
and the Spirit who makes us holy.
Help us to believe in you and worship you,
as the true faith teaches:
three Persons, eternal in glory,
one God, infinite in majesty.
(We make our prayer) through our Lord.

Blessing
Page 92

The Office may conclude with an antiphon of Our Lady (page 82ff)

Corpus Christi

Introduction
Page 90

Hymn
Page 96

Psalm 109

Christ the Lord is a priest for e - ver. Like Mel - chi - ze - dek of old, Je - sus of - fered bread and wine.

* Omit in verses 5 and 6

1. The Lord's revelation to my Master:
   'Sit on my right;
   your foes I will put beneath your feet.'

2. The Lord will wield from Zion
   your sceptre of power;
   rule in the midst of all your foes.

3. A prince from the day of your birth
   on the holy mountains;
   from the womb before the dawn I begot you.

4. The Lord has sworn an oath and will not change.
   'You are a priest for ever,
   a priest like Melchizedek of old.'

5. The Master standing at your right hand
   will shatter rulers in the day of wrath,

6. He shall drink from the stream by the wayside,
   will stand with head held high.

7. Glory be to the Father and to the Son
      and to the Holy Spirit.
   As it was in the beginning, is now
      and ever shall be.
   World without end. Amen.

Psalm 115

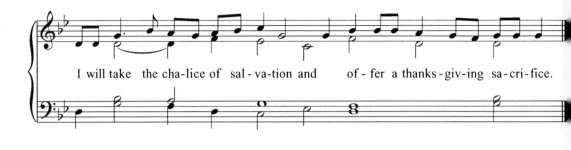

I will take the cha-lice of sal-va-tion and of-fer a thanks-giv-ing sa-cri-fice.

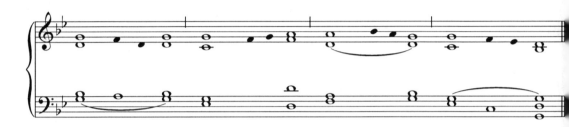

1. I trusted, even <u>when</u> I said:
   'I am sore<u>ly</u> afflicted,'
   and when I said in <u>my</u> alarm:
   'There is no one <u>I</u> can trust.'

2. How can I re<u>pay</u> the Lord
   for his good<u>ness</u> to me?
   The cup of salvation <u>I</u> will raise;
   I will call <u>on</u> the Lord's name.

3. My vows to the Lord I <u>will</u> fulfil
   before <u>all</u> the people.
   O precious in the eyes <u>of</u> the Lord
   is the death <u>of</u> the faithful.

4. Your servant, Lord, your ser<u>vant</u> am I;
   you have loo<u>sened</u> my bonds.
   A thanksgiving sacri<u>fice</u> I make;
   I will call <u>on</u> the Lord's name.

5. My vows to the Lord I <u>will</u> fulfil
   before <u>all</u> the people,
   in the courts of the house <u>of</u> the Lord,
   in your midst, <u>O</u> Jerusalem.

6. Glory be to the Father and to the Son
     and to the <u>Holy</u> Spirit.
   As it was in the beginning, is now
     and <u>ev</u>er shall be.
   World without <u>end</u>. Amen.

Canticle

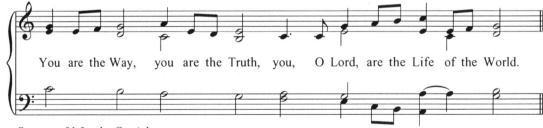

You are the Way, you are the Truth, you, O Lord, are the Life of the World.

See page 91 for the Canticle

50

Reading: 1 Corinthians 11:23-26

For I received from the Lord what I also handed to you, that the Lord
Jesus on the night when he was betrayed took a loaf of bread, and when
he had given thanks, he broke it and said 'This is my body that is for you.
Do this in remembrance of me.' In the same way he took the cup also,
after supper, saying, 'This cup is the new covenant in my blood. Do this,
as often as you drink it, in remembrance of me.' For as often as you eat
this bread and drink the cup, you proclaim the Lord's death until he
comes.

Responsory

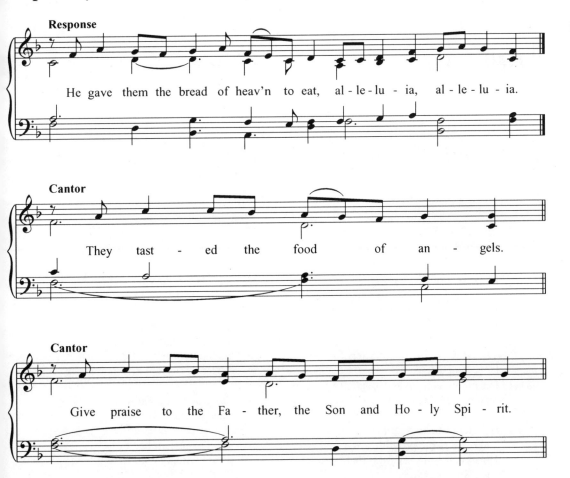

Magnificat

O sac-red feast in which we par-take of Christ: his suf-fer-ings are re-mem-bered, our

minds are filled with grace and we re-ceive a pledge of fu-ture glo-ry. Al-le - lu - ia.

* Omit in verse 4

1. My soul glorifies the Lord,
my spirit rejoices in God, my Saviour.
He looks on his servant in her lowliness;
henceforth all ages will call me blessed.

2. The Almighty works marvels for me.
Holy his name!
His mercy is from age to age,
on those who fear him.

3. He puts forth his arm in strength
and scatters the proud-hearted.
He casts the mighty from their thrones
and raises the lowly.

4. He fills the starving with good things,
sends the rich away empty.

5. He protects Israel, his servant,
remembering his mercy,
the mercy promised to our fathers,
to Abraham and his sons for ever.

6. Glory be to the Father and to the Son
and to the Holy Spirit.
As it was in the beginning, is now
and ever shall be.
World without end. Amen.

Intercessions

Leader   In peace let us pray to the Lord.
As we celebrate Christ's presence in the most holy Eucharist,
we pray that we may receive the Bread of Life with humility
and joy, so that we may grow in holiness and love.

All *(sung after each Intercession)*

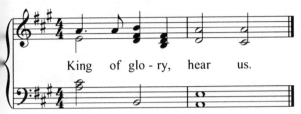

King   of glo - ry,   hear   us.

Leader   We pray that the sick and housebound may find strength
and healing through receiving Christ's love in the holy Eucharist.

Leader   May the departed who have received the holy Eucharist faithfully in their
earthly lives, now be raised up by Jesus into eternal life.

Leader   Let us pray to our heavenly Father
in the words the Lord Jesus gave us.

All   Our Father *(pages 80-81)*

Concluding Prayer

Lord Jesus Christ,
you gave your Church an admirable sacrament
as the abiding memorial of your passion.
Teach us so to worship
the sacred mystery of your Body and Blood,
that its redeeming power
may sanctify us always.
Who live and reign with the Father and the Holy Spirit,
God, for ever and ever.

Blessing
Page 92

The Office may conclude with an antiphon of Our Lady (page 82ff)

Sundays in Ordinary Time
Psalter Week 1

Introduction
Page 90

Hymn
Page 96

Psalm 109

* Omit in verses 5 and 6

1. The Lord's revelation to my Master:
   'Sit on my right;
   your foes I will put beneath your feet.'

2. The Lord will wield from Zion
   your sceptre of power;
   rule in the midst of all your foes.

3. A prince from the day of your birth
   on the holy mountains;
   from the womb before the dawn I begot you.

4. The Lord has sworn an oath and will not change.
   'You are a priest for ever,
   a priest like Melchizedek of old.'

5. The Master standing at your right hand
   will shatter rulers in the day of wrath,

6. He shall drink from the stream by the wayside,
   will stand with head held high.

7. Glory be to the Father and to the Son
   and to the Holy Spirit.
   As it was in the beginning, is now
   and ever shall be.
   World without end. Amen.

Psalm 113a

The earth trem - bled be - fore the Lord, al - le - lu - ia.

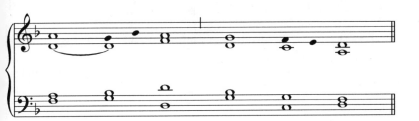

1. When Israel came <u>forth</u> from Egypt,
   Jacob's family from an <u>a</u>lien people,
   Judah became <u>the</u> Lord's temple,
   Israel be<u>came</u> God's kingdom.

2. The sea fled <u>at</u> the sight,
   the Jordan turned back <u>on</u> its course,
   the mountains <u>leapt</u> like rams
   and the hills like <u>year</u>ling sheep.

3. Why was it, sea, <u>that</u> you fled,
   that you turned back, Jordan, <u>on</u> your course?
   Mountains, that you <u>leapt</u> like rams;
   hills, like <u>year</u>ling sheep?

4. Tremble, O earth, be<u>fore</u> the Lord,
   in the presence of the <u>God</u> of Jacob,
   who turns the rock in<u>to</u> a pool
   and flint into a <u>spring</u> of water.

5. Glory be to the Father and to the Son
   and to the <u>Ho</u>ly Spirit.
   As it was in the beginning, is now
   and <u>e</u>ver shall be.
   World without <u>end</u>. Amen.

Canticle (Revelation 19:1-2, 5-7)

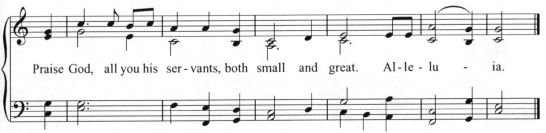

Praise God, all you his ser - vants, both small and great. Al-le - lu - ia.

See page 91 for the Canticle

Reading: 2 Corinthians 1:3-4

Blessed be the God and Father of our Lord Jesus Christ, the Father
of mercies and the God of all consolation, who consoles us in all
our affliction, so that we may be able to console those who are in
any affliction with the consolation with which we ourselves are
consoled by God.

Responsory

Response

Bles - sed are you, O Lord, in the vault of heav'n.

Cantor

You are ex - alt - ed and glo - ri - fied a - bove all else for e - ver.

Cantor

Praise the Fa - ther, the Son and Ho - ly Spi - rit.

Magnificat

The Baptism of the Lord and the beginning of Ordinary Time

The Spi - rit of the Lord rests on me; he has sent

me to preach the Good News to the poor.

During Ordinary Time

Wher - e - ver your trea - sure is, there will your heart be al - so.

The last week of Ordinary Time

Your en - du - rance will win you your lives, · says the Lord.

*

* Omit in verse 4

1. My soul glorifies the Lord,
   my spirit rejoices in God, my Saviour.
   He looks on his servant in her lowliness;
   henceforth all ages will call me blessed.

2. The Almighty works marvels for me.
   Holy his name!
   His mercy is from age to age,
   on those who fear him.

3. He puts forth his arm in strength
   and scatters the proud-hearted.
   He casts the mighty from their thrones
   and raises the lowly.

4. He fills the starving with good things,
   sends the rich away empty.

5. He protects Israel, his servant,
   remembering his mercy,
   the mercy promised to our fathers,
   to Abraham and his sons for ever.

6. Glory be to the Father and to the Son
     and to the Holy Spirit.
   As it was in the beginning, is now
     and ever shall be.
   World without end. Amen.

Intercessions

Leader   In peace let us pray to the Lord.
Lord, may our world resound with your truth,
show forth your compassion, and be at peace
through your spirit.

All *(sung after each Intercession)*

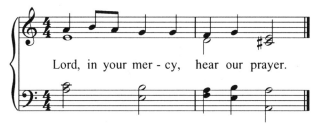

Lord, in your mer - cy,   hear our prayer.

Leader   We pray for all who are homeless today:
we pray for families searching for a place to live
and for refugees driven from their homeland.

Leader   Father, the world is torn by war and hatred;
grant to all peoples the peace your Son came to give.

Leader   Let us pray to our heavenly Father
in the words the Lord Jesus gave us.

All   Our Father *(pages 80-81)*

Concluding Prayer
Either this prayer or the proper prayer for the Sunday from the Breviary

Stay with us, Lord Jesus, as evening falls:
be our companion on our way.
In your mercy inflame our hearts and raise our hope,
so that, in union with our brethren,
we may recognize you in the scriptures,
and in the breaking of Bread.
Who live and reign with the Father and the Holy Spirit,
God, for ever and ever.

Blessing
Page 92

The Office may conclude with an antiphon of Our Lady (page 82ff)

Sundays in Ordinary Time
Psalter Week 2

Introduction
Page 90

Hymn
Page 96

Psalm 109

Christ the Lord is a priest for e - ver ac - cord - ing to the or - der of Mel - chi - sa - dek. Al - le - lu - ia.

* Omit in verses 5 and 6

1. The Lord's revelation <u>to</u> my Master:
   'Sit <u>on</u> my right;
   your foes I will put be<u>neath</u> your feet.'

2. The Lord will <u>wield</u> from Zion
   your scep<u>tre</u> of power;
   rule in the midst of <u>all</u> your foes.

3. A prince from the day <u>of</u> your birth
   on the <u>holy</u> mountains;
   from the womb before the dawn <u>I</u> begot you.

4. The Lord has sworn an oath and <u>will</u> not change.
   'You are a <u>priest</u> for ever,
   a priest like Melchize<u>dek</u> of old.'

5. The Master standing <u>at</u> your right hand
   will shatter rulers in the <u>day</u> of wrath,

6. He shall drink from the stream <u>by</u> the wayside,
   will stand with <u>head</u> held high.

7. Glory be to the Father and to the Son
   and to the <u>Holy</u> Spirit.
   As it was in the beginning, is now
   and <u>ever</u> shall be.
   World without <u>end</u>. Amen.

Psalm 113b

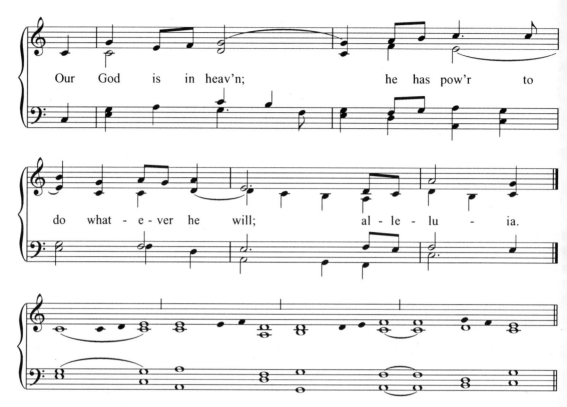

Our God is in heav'n; he has pow'r to do what - e - ver he will; al - le - lu - ia.

1. Not to us, Lord, not to us,
   but to your name give the glory
   for the sake of your love and your truth,
   lest the heathen say: 'Where is their God?'

2. But our God is in the heavens;
   whatever God wills, God does.
   Their idols are silver and gold,
   the work of human hands.

3. They have mouths but they cannot speak;
   they have eyes but they cannot see;
   they have ears but they cannot hear;
   they have nostrils but they cannot smell.

4. With their hands they cannot feel;
      with their feet they cannot walk.
   (No sound comes from their throats.)
   Their makers will come to be like them
   and so will all who trust in them.

5. Israel's family, trust in the Lord;
   he is your help and your shield.
   Aaron's family, trust in the Lord;
   he is your help and your shield.

6. You who fear the Lord, trust in the Lord;
   he is your help and your shield.
   The Lord remembers and will bless us;
   will bless the family of Israel.
      (will bless the family of Aaron.)

7. The Lord will bless those who fear him,
   the little no less than the great;
   to you may the Lord grant increase,
   to you and all your children.

8. May you be blessed by the Lord,
   the maker of heaven and earth.
   The heavens belong to the Lord
   but to us God has given the earth.

9. The dead shall not praise the Lord,
   nor those who go down into the silence.
   But we who live bless the Lord
   now and for ever. Amen.

10. Glory be to the Father and to the Son
       and to the Holy Spirit.
    As it was in the beginning, is now
       and ever shall be.
    World without end. Amen.

Canticle (Revelation 19:1-2, 5-7)

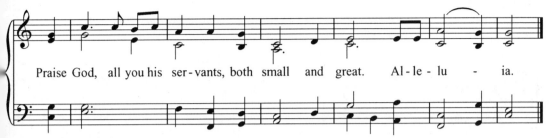

Praise God, all you his servants, both small and great. Al-le-lu-ia.

See page 91 for the Canticle

Reading: 2 Thessalonians 2:13-14

But we must always give thanks to God for you, brothers and sisters beloved by the Lord, because God chose you as the first for salvation through sanctification by the Spirit and through belief in the truth. For this purpose he called you through our proclamation of the good news, so that you may obtain the glory of our Lord Jesus Christ.

Responsory

Response

Great is our Lord, great is his might.

Cantor

His wis-dom can ne-ver be meas-ured.

Cantor

Praise the Fa-ther, the Son and Ho-ly Spi-rit.

Magnificat

Additional antiphons for the Baptism of the Lord and the beginnning of Ordinary Time and the last weeks of Ordinary Time may be found on pages 56-57.

Ask and you will re - ceive; seek and you will find; knock and the door will be o - pened to you. Al - le - lu - ia.

or

Who - e - ver does not take up the cross and fol - low me, can - not be my dis - ci - ple, says the Lord.

*

* Omit in verse 4

1. My soul glorifies the Lord,
   my spirit rejoices in <u>God</u>, my Saviour.
   He looks on his servant <u>in</u> her lowliness;
   henceforth all ages will <u>call</u> me blessed.

2. The Almighty works mar<u>vels</u> for me.
   Ho<u>ly</u> his name!
   His mercy is from <u>age</u> to age,
   on <u>those</u> who fear him.

3. He puts forth his <u>arm</u> in strength
   and scatters <u>the</u> proud-hearted.
   He casts the mighty <u>from</u> their thrones
   and rai<u>ses</u> the lowly.

4. He fills the starving <u>with</u> good things,
   sends the rich <u>a</u>way empty.

5. He protects Isra<u>el</u>, his servant,
   remember<u>ing</u> his mercy,
   the mercy promised <u>to</u> our fathers,
   to Abraham and his <u>sons</u> for ever.

6. Glory be . . .

Intercessions

Leader   In peace let us pray to the Lord.
   We pray for all nations: may they seek the way that
   leads to peace, respect each person's rights and freedoms
   and share generously the world's resources.

All *(sung after each Intercession)*

In - to   your   hands   we   com - mend   our   prayers.

Leader   Lord, you prayed that your followers might all
   be one; give us the will to search for unity
   and inspire us to work and pray together.

Leader   Lord, we pray for those who have died in your
   friendship and give thanks for their lives;
   may they rest in the peace of eternity.

Leader   Let us pray to our heavenly Father
   in the words the Lord Jesus gave us.

All   Our Father *(pages 80-81)*

Concluding Prayer
Either this prayer or the proper prayer for the Sunday from the Breviary

Almighty God,
ruler of all things in heaven and on earth,
listen favourably to the prayer of your people,
and grant us your peace in our day.
We make our prayer through our Lord Jesus Christ, your Son,
who lives and reigns with you and the Holy Spirit,
God, for ever and ever.

Blessing
Page 92

The Office may conclude with an antiphon of Our Lady (page 82ff)

Sundays in Ordinary Time
Psalter Week 3

Introduction
Page 90

Hymn
Page 96

Psalm 109

The Lord's re-ve-la-tion to my Mas-ter: '*Sit on my right.' Al-le-lu - ia.*

* Omit in verses 5 and 6

1. The Lord's revelation <u>to</u> my Master:
   'Sit <u>on</u> my right;
   your foes I will put be<u>neath</u> your feet.'

2. The Lord will <u>wield</u> from Zion
   your scep<u>tre</u> of power;
   rule in the midst of <u>all</u> your foes.

3. A prince from the day <u>of</u> your birth
   on the <u>holy</u> mountains;
   from the womb before the dawn <u>I</u> begot you.

4. The Lord has sworn an oath and <u>will</u> not change.
   'You are a <u>priest</u> for ever,
   a priest like Melchize<u>dek</u> of old.'

5. The Master standing <u>at</u> your right hand
   will shatter rulers in the <u>day</u> of wrath,

6. He shall drink from the stream <u>by</u> the wayside
   will stand with <u>head</u> held high.

7. Glory be to the Father and to the Son
   and to the <u>Holy</u> Spirit.
   As it was in the beginning, is now
   and <u>ever</u> shall be.
   World without <u>end</u>. Amen.

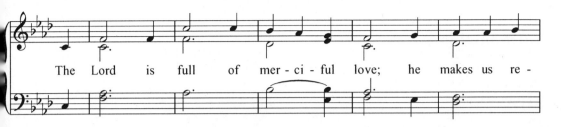

The Lord is full of mer - ci - ful love; he makes us re -

mem - ber his won - ders, al - le - lu - ia.

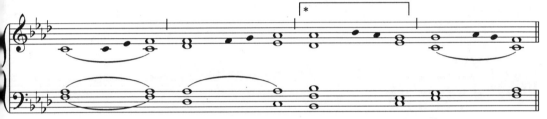

*

Omit in verses 5 and 6

1. I will thank the Lord with all my heart
   in the meeting of the just and their assembly.
   Great are the works of the Lord,
   to be pondered by all who love them.

2. Majestic and glorious God's work,
   whose justice stands firm for ever.
   God makes us remember these wonders.
   The Lord is compassion and love.

3. God gives food to those who fear him;
   keeps his covenant ever in mind;
   shows mighty works to his people
   by giving them the land of the nations.

4. God's works are justice and truth,
   God's precepts are all of them sure,
   standing firm for ever and ever;
   they are made in uprightness and truth.

5. God has sent deliverance to his people
   and established his covenant for ever.
   Holy is God's name, to be feared.

6. To fear the Lord is the first stage of wisdom;
   all who do so prove themselves wise.
   God's praise shall last for ever!

7. Glory be to the Father and to the Son
      and to the Holy Spirit.
   As it was in the beginning, is now
      and ever shall be.
   World without end. Amen.

Canticle

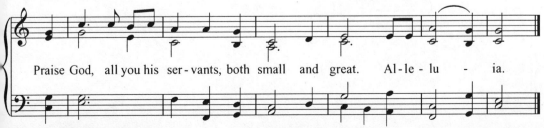

Praise God, all you his ser - vants, both small and great. Al - le - lu - ia.

See page 91 for the Canticle

Reading: 1 Peter 1:3-5

Blessed be the God and Father of our Lord Jesus Christ! By his great
mercy he has given us a new birth into a living hope through the resurrection
of Jesus Christ from the dead, and into an inheritance that is imperishable,
undefiled, and unfading, kept in heaven for you, who are being protected
by the power of God through faith for a salvation ready to be revealed in
the last time.

Responsory

Response

Bles - sed are you, O Lord, in the vault of heav'n.

Cantor

You are ex - alt - ed and glo - ri - fied a - bove all else for e - ver.

Cantor

Praise the Fa - ther, the Son and Ho - ly Spi - rit.

Magnificat

The Baptism of the Lord and the beginning of Ordinary Time

The Spi - rit of the Lord rests on me; he has sent

me to preach the Good News to the poor.

During Ordinary Time

Wher - e - ver your trea - sure is, there will your heart be al - so.

The last week of Ordinary Time

Your en - du - rance will win you your lives, says the Lord.

* *Omit in verse 4*

1. My soul glorifies the Lord,
   my spirit rejoices in God, my Saviour.
   He looks on his servant in her lowliness;
   henceforth all ages will call me blessed.

2. The Almighty works marvels for me.
   Holy his name!
   His mercy is from age to age,
   on those who fear him.

3. He puts forth his arm in strength
   and scatters the proud-hearted.
   He casts the mighty from their thrones
   and raises the lowly.

4. He fills the starving with good things,
   sends the rich away empty.

5. He protects Israel, his servant,
   remembering his mercy,
   the mercy promised to our fathers,
   to Abraham and his sons for ever.

6. Glory be to the Father and to the Son
      and to the Holy Spirit.
   As it was in the beginning, is now
      and ever shall be.
   World without end. Amen.

Intercessions

Leader In peace let us pray to the Lord.
Lord, we pray for all those who suffer
or are overburdened; may they feel
your presence in their pain.

All *(sung after each Intercession)*

Show us, Lord, the path of life.

Leader Father, we entrust those who have died
to your everlasting care and ask you to
comfort those who mourn their loss.

Leader We pray for our families and the community
in which we live and work; may we find you
in them.

Leader Let us pray to our heavenly Father
in the words the Lord Jesus gave us.

All   Our Father *(pages 80-81)*

Concluding Prayer
Either this prayer or the proper prayer for the Sunday from the Breviary

Guard your family, Lord, with constant loving care, for in your divine
grace we place our only hope. We make our prayer through our Lord
Jesus Christ, your Son, who lives and reigns with you and the Holy Spirit,
God, for ever and ever.

Blessing
Page 92

The Office may conclude with an antiphon of Our Lady (page 82ff)

Sundays in Ordinary Time
Psalter Week 4

Introduction
Page 90

Hymn
Page 96

Psalm 109

In ho-ly splen-dour I be-got you be-fore the dawn, al-le-lu - ia.

* Omit in verses 5 and 6

1. The Lord's revelation <u>to</u> my Master:
   'Sit <u>on</u> my right;
   your foes I will put be<u>neath</u> your feet.'

2. The Lord will <u>wield</u> from Zion
   your scep<u>tre</u> of power;
   rule in the midst of <u>all</u> your foes.

3. A prince from the day <u>of</u> your birth
   on the <u>holy</u> mountains;
   from the womb before the dawn <u>I</u> begot you.

4. The Lord has sworn an oath and <u>will</u> not change.
   'You are a <u>priest</u> for ever,
   a priest like Melchize<u>dek</u> of old.'

5. The Master standing <u>at</u> your right hand
   will shatter rulers in the <u>day</u> of wrath,

6. He shall drink from the stream <u>by</u> the wayside,
   will stand with <u>head</u> held high.

7. Glory be to the Father and to the Son
      and to the <u>Holy</u> Spirit.
   As it was in the beginning, is now
      and <u>ever</u> shall be.
   World without <u>end</u>. Amen.

Psalm 111

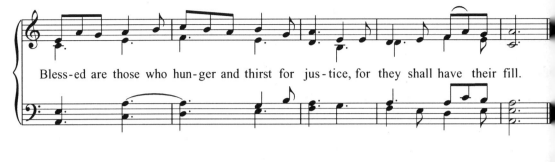

Bless-ed are those who hun-ger and thirst for jus-tice, for they shall have their fill.

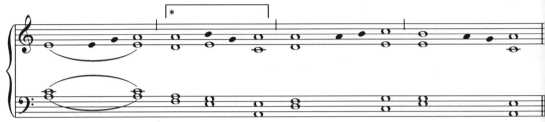

* Omit in verses 5 and 6

1. Happy are those who <u>fear</u> the Lord,
   who take delight in all <u>God's</u> commands.
   Their descendants shall be power<u>ful</u> on earth;
   the children of the up<u>right</u> are blessed.

2. Wealth and riches are <u>in</u> their homes;
   their justice stands <u>firm</u> for ever.
   They are lights in the darkness <u>for</u> the upright;
   they are generous, merci<u>ful</u> and just.

3. Good people take pi<u>ty</u> and lend,
   they conduct their af<u>fairs</u> with honour.
   The just will <u>never</u> waver,
   they will be remem<u>bered</u> for ever.

4. They have no fear of <u>evil</u> news;
   with firm hearts they trust <u>in</u> the Lord.
   With steadfast hearts they <u>will</u> not fear;
   they will see the downfall <u>of</u> their foes.

5. Openhanded, they give <u>to</u> the poor;
   their justice stands <u>firm</u> for ever.
   Their heads will be <u>raised</u> in glory.

6. The wicked shall see this <u>and</u> be angry,
   shall grind their teeth and <u>pine</u> away;
   the desires of the wicked <u>lead</u> to doom.

7. Glory be to the Father and to the son
   and to the <u>Holy</u> Spirit.
   As it was in the beginning, is now
   and <u>ever</u> shall be.
   World without <u>end</u>. Amen.

Canticle (Revelation 19:1-2, 5-7)

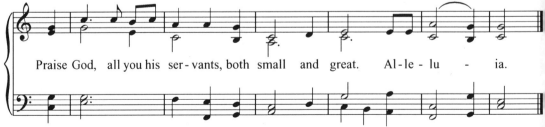

Praise God, all you his ser-vants, both small and great. Al-le-lu - ia.

See page 91 for the Canticle

ading: Hebrews 12:22-24

you have come to Mount Zion and to the city of the living God, the
venly Jerusalem, and to innumerable angels in festal gathering, and to
assembly of the firstborn who are enrolled in heaven, and to God the
ge of all, and to the spirits of the righteous made perfect, and to Jesus,
mediator of a new covenant, and to the sprinkled blood that speaks a
ter word than the blood of Abel.

esponsory

Great is our Lord, great is his might.

His wis-dom can ne-ver be meas-ured.

Praise the Fa-ther, the Son and Ho-ly Spi-rit.

Magnificat

*Additional antiphons for the Baptism of the Lord and the beginning of Ordinary Time
and the last weeks of Ordinary Time may be found on pages 56-57.*

Ask and you will re-ceive; seek and you will find; knock and the door will be o - pened to you. Al - le - lu - ia.

or

Who - e - ver does not take up the cross and fol - low me, can - not be my dis - ci - ple, says the Lord.

* Omit in verse 4

1. My soul glorifies the Lord,
   my spirit rejoices in God, my Saviour.
   He looks on his servant in her lowliness;
   henceforth all ages will call me blessed.

2. The Almighty works marvels for me.
   Holy his name!
   His mercy is from age to age,
   on those who fear him.

3. He puts forth his <u>arm</u> in strength
   and scatters <u>the</u> proud-hearted.
   He casts the mighty <u>from</u> their thrones
   and rai<u>ses</u> the lowly.

4. He fills the starving <u>with</u> good things,
   sends the rich <u>a</u>way empty.

5. He protects Isra<u>el</u>, his servant,
   remember<u>ing</u> his mercy,
   the mercy promised <u>to</u> our fathers,
   to Abraham and his <u>sons</u> for ever.

6. Glory be . . .

Intercessions

Leader In peace let us pray to the Lord.
May the Church hear the Word of God with humility and joy,
and so bear fruit in abundance.

All *(sung after each Intercession)*

Lord   of love,   may your   king - dom   come.

Leader May justice and peace flourish in our neighbourhood, in this country
and in the world. May the Lord raise up leaders who are happy
to serve and protect them from power's corruption.

Leader We pray for children and young people. May the Lord protect
them from all evil and strengthen them in faith.

Leader Let us pray to our heavenly Father
in the words the Lord Jesus gave us.

All   Our Father *(pages 80-81)*

Concluding Prayer

Either this prayer or the proper prayer for the Sunday from the Breviary

We give you thanks, Lord God Almighty,
for bringing us safely to the evening of this day;
we humbly ask that the prayer we make with uplifted hands
may be an offering pleasing in your sight.
We make our prayer through our Lord Jesus Christ, your Son,
who lives and reigns with you and the Holy Spirit,
God, for ever and ever.
Amen.

Blessing

Page 92

The Office may conclude with an antiphon of Our Lady (page 82ff)

The Blessed Virgin Mary

Introduction
Page 90

Hymn
Page 96

Psalm 121

Hail Ma-ry, full of grace, the Lord is with you. Al - le - lu - ia.

Eastertime

1. I rejoiced when I <u>heard</u> them say:
   'Let us go <u>to</u> God's house.'
   And now our <u>feet</u> are standing
   within your gates, <u>O</u> Jerusalem.

2. Jerusalem is built <u>as</u> a city
   strong<u>ly</u> compact.
   It is there that the <u>tribes</u> go up,
   the tribes <u>of</u> the Lord.

3. For Israel's <u>law</u> it is,
   there to praise <u>the</u> Lord's name.
   There were set the <u>thrones</u> of judgement
   of the <u>house</u> of David.

4. For the peace of Jeru<u>sa</u>lem pray:
   'Peace be <u>to</u> your homes!
   May peace reign <u>in</u> your walls,
   in your pa<u>la</u>ces, peace!'

5. For the love of my fami<u>ly</u> and friends
   I say: 'Peace <u>up</u>on you.'
   For love of the house <u>of</u> the Lord
   I will ask <u>for</u> your good.

6. Glory be to the Father and to the Son
   and to the <u>Holy</u> Spirit.
   As it was in the beginning, is now
   and <u>ev</u>er shall be.
   World without <u>end</u>. Amen.

Psalm 126

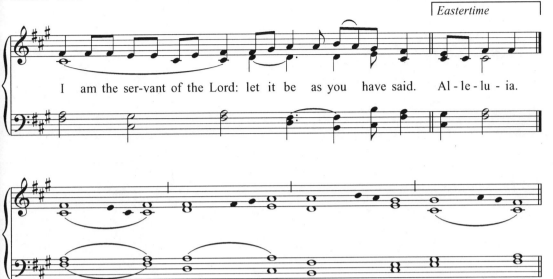

I am the ser-vant of the Lord: let it be as you have said. Al - le - lu - ia.

1. If the Lord does not <u>build</u> the house,
   in vain do its <u>buil</u>ders labour;
   if the Lord does not watch o<u>ver</u> the city,
   in vain do the wat<u>chers</u> keep vigil.

2. In vain is your <u>ear</u>lier rising,
   your going la<u>ter</u> to rest,
   you who toil for the <u>bread</u> you eat,
   when God pours gifts on the beloved <u>while</u> they slumber.

3. Yes, children are a gift <u>from</u> the Lord,
   a blessing, the fruit <u>of</u> the womb.
   The sons and daugh<u>ters</u> of youth
   are like arrows in the hand <u>of</u> a warrior.

4. O the happi<u>ness</u> of those
   who have filled their quiver <u>with</u> these arrows!
   They will have no <u>cause</u> for shame
   when they dispute with their foes <u>in</u> the gateways.

5. Glory be to the Father and to the Son
   and to the <u>Ho</u>ly Spirit.
   As it was in the beginning, is now
   and <u>ev</u>er shall be.
   World without <u>end</u>. Amen.

Canticle (Ephesians 1:3-10)

You are the most bless'd of all wo - men and

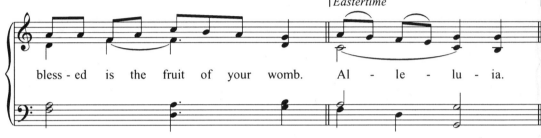

bless - ed is the fruit of your womb. Al - le - lu - ia.

Eastertime

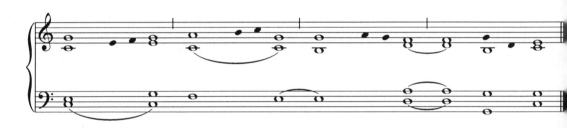

1. Blessed be the God and Father
   of our Lord Jesus Christ,
   who has blessed us in Christ
   with every spiritual blessing
   in the heavenly places.

2. He chose us in him
   before the foundation of the world,
   that we should be holy
   and blameless before him.

3. He destined us in love to be his children
   through Jesus Christ,
   according to the purpose of his will
   to the praise of his glorious grace
   which he freely bestowed on us in the Beloved.

4. In him we have redemption through his blood,
   the forgiveness of our trespasses,
   according to the riches of his grace
   which he lavished upon us.

5. He has made known to us
   in all wisdom and insight
   the mystery of his will,
   according to his purpose
   which he set forth in Christ.

6. His purpose he set forth in Christ,
   as a plan for the fullness of time,
   to unite all things in him,
   things in heaven and things on earth.

7. Glory be to the Father and to the Son
   and to the Holy Spirit.
   As it was in the beginning, is now
   and ever shall be.
   World without end. Amen.

Reading: Galatians 4:4-5

But when the fullness of time had come, God sent his Son, born of a woman, born under the law, in order to redeem those who were under the law, so that we might receive adoption as children.

Responsory

Response

Hail Ma - ry, full of grace, the Lord is with you. Al - le - lu - ia, al - le - lu - ia.

Eastertime

Cantor

Bles-sed are you a-mong wo-men and bles-sed is the fruit of your womb.

Cantor

Praise the Fa - ther, the Son and Ho - ly Spi - rit.

Magnificat

He has looked with mer - cy on his hum - ble ser - vant, for

now all ge - ne - ra - tions will call me bles - sed.

*Omit in verse 4

* Omit in verse 4

1. My soul glorifies the Lord,
   my spirit rejoices in God, my Saviour.
   He looks on his servant in her lowliness;
   henceforth all ages will call me blessed.

2. The Almighty works marvels for me.
   Holy his name!
   His mercy is from age to age,
   on those who fear him.

3. He puts forth his arm in strength
   and scatters the proud-hearted.
   He casts the mighty from their thrones
   and raises the lowly.

4. He fills the starving with good things,
   sends the rich away empty.

5. He protects Israel, his servant,
   remembering his mercy,
   the mercy promised to our fathers,
   to Abraham and his sons for ever.

6. Glory be to the Father and to the Son
      and to the Holy Spirit.
   As it was in the beginning, is now
      and ever shall be.
   World without end. Amen.

See also pages 7 or 12 (Magnificat for Advent)

Intercessions

Leader   In peace let us pray to the Lord.
Lord, teach us to respond to your will as
Mary did; may your word bear fruit in us.

All *(sung after each Intercession)*

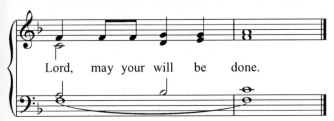

Lord, may your will be done.

Leader   Father, your Son Jesus gave Mary his mother to the Church;
may we accept your word in faith as she did.

Leader   Father, Mary listened to your voice and brought your word
into the world; by answering your call may we too bring
your Son to all whom we meet.

Leader   Let us pray to our heavenly Father
in the words the Lord Jesus gave us.

All   Our Father *(pages 80-81)*

Concluding Prayer

Let the gracious intercession of Blessed Mary
ever-Virgin help us, Lord: may she protect us
in all dangers and make us rejoice in your peace.
We make our prayer through our Lord Jesus Christ,
your Son, who lives and reigns with you and the Holy Spirit,
one God, for ever and ever.

Blessing
Page 92

The Office may conclude with an antiphon of Our Lady (page 82ff)

The Lord's Prayer

First setting

Second setting

Our Fa-ther, who art in hea-ven, hal-lowed be thy name; thy king-dom come;

thy will be done on earth as it is in hea-ven. Give us this day our dai-ly bread;

and for-give us our tres-pas-ses as we for-give those who tres-pass a-gainst us;

and lead us not in-to temp-ta-tion, but de-li-ver us from e-vil.

Doxology

For the king-dom, the pow'r, and the glo-ry are yours, now and for e-ver. A-men.

Music: Nicolai Rimsky-Korsakov (1844-1908) based on traditional Russian Orthodox sources,
adapted by Joseph Gelineau and Robert B Kelly (b.1948)

Antiphons of Our Lady

Mother of Christ

Mother of Christ! now hear your peo-ple's cry,
star of the deep and por-tal of the sky!
Mo-ther of him who you from no-thing made,
sink-ing we strive and call to you for aid.
Oh, by the joy which Ga-briel brought to you, blest
vir-gin first and last, your mer-cy let us see.

Text: *Alma Redemptoris Mater*, Hermann the Lame (d.1054) trans. unknown
Music: Alan Rees

Alma redemptoris mater

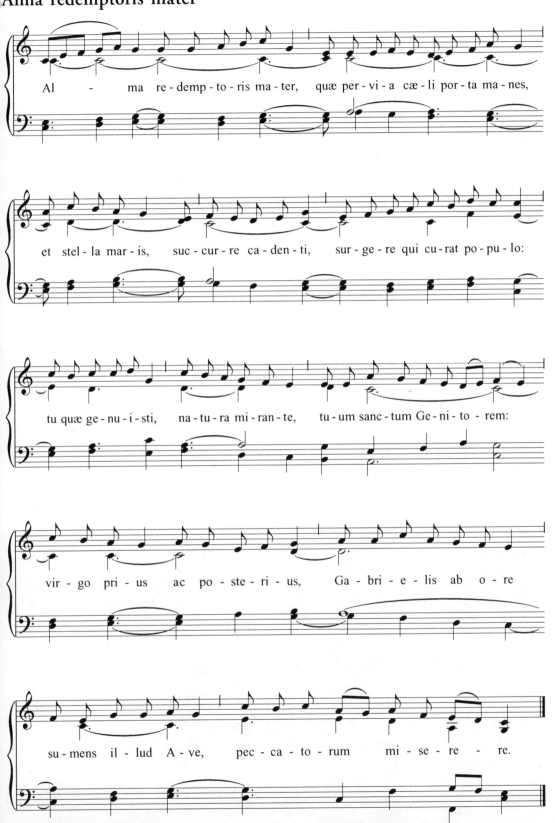

Al - ma re-demp-to-ris ma-ter, quæ per-vi-a cæ-li por-ta ma-nes,

et stel-la mar-is, suc-cur-re ca-den-ti, sur-ge-re qui cu-rat po-pu-lo:

tu quæ ge-nu-i-sti, na-tu-ra mi-ran-te, tu-um sanc-tum Ge-ni-to-rem:

vir-go pri-us ac po-ste-ri-us, Ga-bri-e-lis ab o-re

su-mens il-lud A - ve, pec-ca-to-rum mi-se-re - re.

Text: Hermann the Lame (d.1054)
Music: Plainsong, accompaniment by Gregory Murray (1905-1992) revised by Andrew Moore

Hail, Queen of heaven

Hail, Queen of heav'n be - yond com - pare, to whom the an - gels hom - age pay;

hail, root of Jes - se, gate of light, that op - ened for the world's new day.

Re - joice, O Vir - gin un - sur - passed, in whom our ran - som has be - gun,

for all your lov - ing child - ren pray to Christ, our Sa - viour and your Son.

Text: *Alma Redemptoris Mater,* Hermann the Lame (d.1054) trans. unknown
Music: Alan Rees

Ave, Regina cælorum

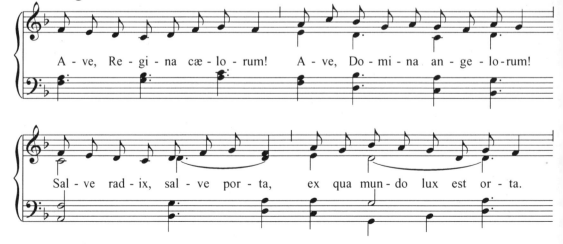

A - ve, Re - gi - na cæ - lo - rum! A - ve, Do - mi - na an - ge - lo - rum!

Sal - ve rad - ix, sal - ve por - ta, ex qua mun - do lux est or - ta.

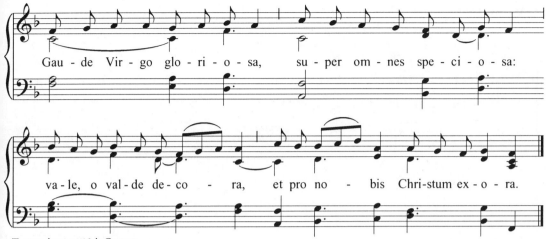

Gau - de Vir - go glo - ri - o - sa, su - per om - nes spe - ci - o - sa: va - le, o val - de de - co - ra, et pro no - bis Chri-stum ex - o - ra.

Text: unknown, 12th Century
Music: Plainsong, accompaniment by Andrew Moore

During Eastertime

All joy is yours

All joy is yours, O Queen of heav'n, al - le - lu - ia, for Christ the Child of your pure womb, al - le - lu - ia, is ri - sen as he pro - mised us, al - le - lu - ia, so pray for us to God, al - le - lu - ia, al - le - lu - ia, al - le - lu - ia.

Text: unknown, 12th century, trans. James Quinn
Music: Alan Rees

Regina cæli

Re-gi-nacæ-li, læ-ta-re, al-le-lu-ia, qui-a quem me-ru-i-sti por-ta-re, al-le-lu-ia,

re-sur-re-xit si-cut di-xit, al-le-lu-ia, O-ra pro no-bis De-um, al-le-lu-ia.

Text: unknown, 12th century
Music: Plainsong arr. Andrew Moore

During Ordinary Time
Hail, holy queen

Hail, ho-ly queen, Mo-ther of mer-cy! Hail, our life, our sweet-ness and our hope!

To you do we cry, poor ban-ished child-ren of Eve;

to you do we send up our sighs, mourn-ing and weep-ing in this vale of tears.

Turn then, most gra-cious ad - vo-cate, your eyes of mer-cy to-wards us; and af-ter

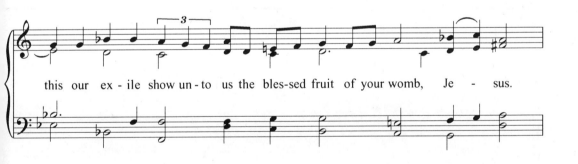

this our ex - ile show un-to us the bles-sed fruit of your womb, Je - sus.

O cle - ment; O lov - ing; O sweet vir - gin Ma - ry.

Text: Hermann the Lame (d.1054) trans. unknown
Music: Alan Rees

Salve, Regina

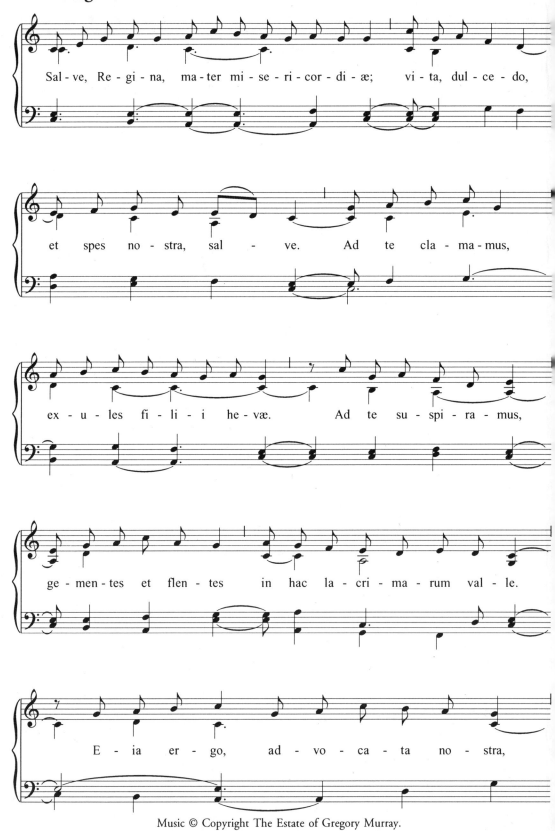

Sal - ve, Re - gi - na, ma - ter mi - se - ri - cor - di - æ; vi - ta, dul - ce - do,

et spes no - stra, sal - ve. Ad te cla - ma - mus,

ex - u - les fi - li - i he - væ. Ad te su - spi - ra - mus,

ge - men - tes et flen - tes in hac la - cri - ma - rum val - le.

E - ia er - go, ad - vo - ca - ta no - stra,

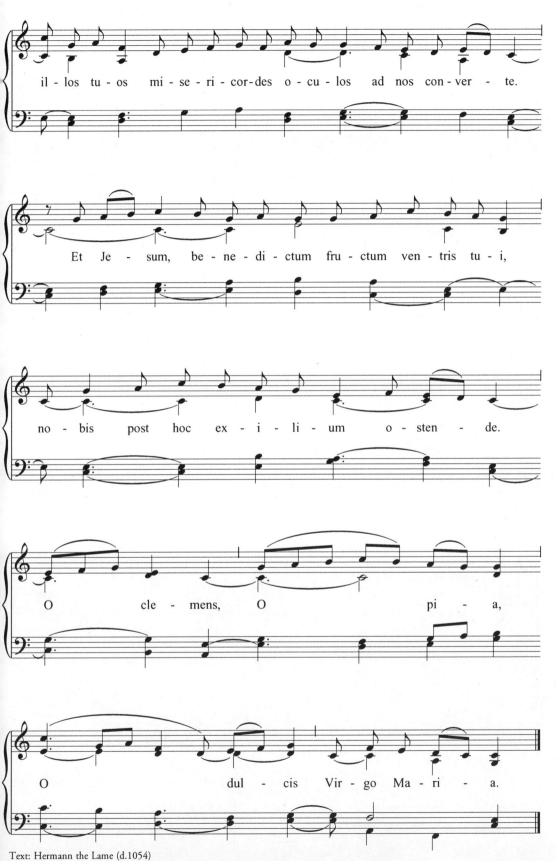

il - los tu - os mi - se - ri - cor-des o - cu - los ad nos con - ver - te.

Et Je - sum, be - ne - di -ctum fru - ctum ven - tris tu - i,

no - bis post hoc ex - i - li - um o - sten - de.

O cle - mens, O pi - a,

O dul - cis Vir - go Ma - ri - a.

Text: Hermann the Lame (d.1054)
Music: Plainsong, accompaniment by Gregory Murray (1905-1992) revised by Andrew Moore

Common texts for the Introduction, Canticle and Dismissal

Introduction

O God, come to our aid. O Lord, make haste to help us!

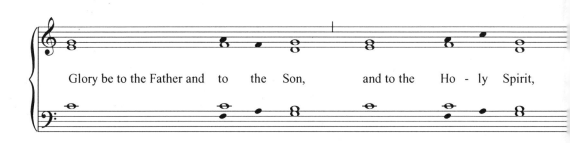

Glory be to the Father and to the Son, and to the Ho - ly Spirit,

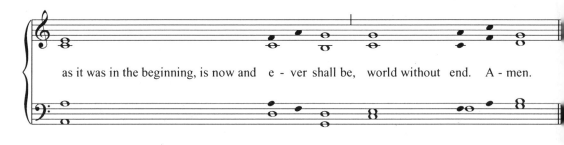

as it was in the beginning, is now and e - ver shall be, world without end. A - men.

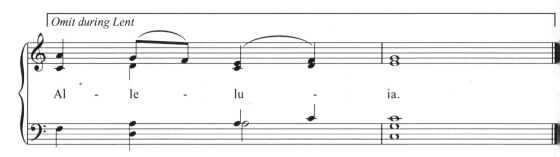

Omit during Lent

Al - le - lu - ia.

Canticle

See the appropriate Sunday for the Antiphon

All

Al - le - lu - ia.

Cantor/Choir

1. Salvation and power and glory belong to our God,
2. Praise our God, all you his servants,
3. The Lord our God, the almighty, reigns,
4. The marriage of the Lamb has come,

All

Al - le - lu - ia.

Cantor/Choir

his judgements are true and just.
you who fear him small and great.
let us rejoice and exult and give him the glory.
and his bride has made her - self ready.

All

Al - le - lu - ia, al - le - lu - ia.

Cantor/Choir

Glory be to the Father, and to the Son, and to the Holy Spirit,

as it was in the beginning, is now, and ever shall be, world without end. A - men.

Repeat Antiphon (see appropriate Sunday)

91

The Blessing and Dismissal

When a priest or deacon presides over the Office

The Lord be with you.
And also with you.
May almighty God bless you, the Father, the Son, and the Holy Spirit.
Amen.

When no priest or deacon is present

The Lord bless us, and keep us from all evil, and bring us to everlasting life.
Amen.

Then:

or

Psalms which may be used
instead of Psalm 109

Psalm 92

Ho - li - ness is fit - ting to your house,   O Lord, un - til the   end   of   time.

1. The Lord is king, with majesty enrobed;
   the Lord is robed with might,
   and girded round with power.

2. The world you made firm, not to be moved;
   your throne has stood firm from of old.
   From all eternity, O Lord, you are.

3. The waters have lifted up, O Lord,
   the waters have lifted up their voice,
   the waters have lifted up their thunder.

4. Greater than the roar of mighty waters,
   more glorious than the surgings of the sea,
   the Lord is glorious on high.

5. Truly your decrees are to be trusted.
   Holiness is fitting to your house,
   O Lord, until the end of time.

6. Glory be to the Father and to the Son
     and to the Holy Spirit.
   As it was in the beginning, is now
     and ever shall be.
   World without end. Amen.

Psalm 95

The Lord is great and wor - thy of all praise.

* Omit in verses 4, 5, 6 and 7

1. The Lord is king, let <u>earth</u> rejoice,
   let all the coast<u>lands</u> be glad.
   Surrounded by <u>cloud</u> and darkness;
   justice and <u>right</u>, God's throne.

2. A fire pre<u>pares</u> the way;
   it burns up foes on <u>every</u> side.
   God's lightnings light <u>up</u> the world,
   the earth trembles <u>at</u> the sight.

3. The mountains <u>melt</u> like wax
   before the Lord of <u>all</u> the earth.
   The skies pro<u>claim</u> God's justice;
   all peoples <u>see</u> God's glory.

4. Let those who serve idols <u>be</u> ashamed,
   those who boast of their <u>worth</u>less gods.
   All you spirits, wor<u>ship</u> the Lord.

5. Zion hears <u>and</u> is glad;
   the people of Ju<u>dah</u> rejoice
   because of your judge<u>ments,</u> O Lord.

6. For you indeed <u>are</u> the Lord
   most high above <u>all</u> the earth,
   exalted far a<u>bove</u> all spirits.

7. The Lord loves those <u>who</u> hate evil,
   guards the souls <u>of</u> the saints,
   and sets them free <u>from</u> the wicked.

8. Light shines forth <u>for</u> the just
   and joy for the up<u>right</u> of heart.
   Rejoice, you just, <u>in</u> the Lord;
   give glory to God's <u>holy</u> name.

9. Glory be to the Father and to the Son
      and to the <u>Holy</u> Spirit.
   As it was in the beginning, is now
      and <u>ever</u> shall be.
   World without <u>end</u>. Amen.

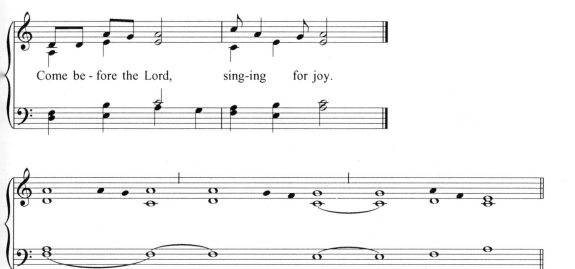

Come be-fore the Lord, sing-ing for joy.

1. Cry out with joy to the Lord, all the earth.
   Serve the Lord with gladness.
   Come before God, singing for joy.

2. Know that the Lord is God,
   our Maker, to whom we belong,
   we are God's people, sheep of the flock.

3. Enter the gates with thanksgiving,
   God's courts with songs of praise.
   Give thanks to God and bless his name.

4. Indeed, how good is the Lord,
   whose merciful love is eternal;
   whose faithfulness lasts for ever.

5. Glory be to the Father and to the Son
      and to the Holy Spirit.
   As it was in the beginning, is now
      and ever shall be.
   World without end. Amen.

Suggested hymns

Ordinary Time
Again the Lord's own day is here
All my hope on God is founded
Be thou my vision
Glory to thee, my God, this night
God hath spoken by his prophets
Holy God, we praise thy name
King of glory, King of peace
Let all the world
Light of our darkness, Word of God
Lord of all hopefulness
Lord, thy word abideth
On this day, the first of days
The day thou gavest, Lord, is ended
Thou, whose almighty word
To God with gladness sing
Worship, glory, praise and honour

Advent
Come, thou long-expected Jesus
Hark, a herald voice is calling
O comfort my people
O come, O come, Emmanuel
On Jordan's bank the baptist's cry
The coming of our God
Wake, O wake, with tidings thrilling

Christmastide
A noble flower of Judah
A child is born in Bethlehem
Let all mortal flesh keep silence
O come, all ye faithful
Of the Father's love begotten
The race that long in darkness pined
Unto us a child is born
What child is this?

Epiphany
As with gladness men of old
Bethlehem, of noblest cities
Hail to the Lord's anointed

Lent
All you who seek a comfort sure
Dear Lord and Father of mankind
Fight the good fight
From the depths we cry to thee
In company with Christians past
Lord, who throughout these forty days
Lord Jesus, think on me

Passsiontide
Faithful cross
Glory be to Jesus
My song is love unknown
O sacred head, ill used

Sing, my tongue, the song of triumph
The royal banners forward go
When I survey the wondrous cross

Eastertide
At the Lamb's high feast
Battle is o'er
Bring, all ye dear-bought nations
Christ the Lord is risen today
Now the green blade riseth
The day of resurrection
Ye sons and daughters of the Lord
Ye choirs of new Jerusalem

Ascensiontide / Christ the King *
Christ triumphant*
Christ is King of earth and heaven*
Christus vincit*
Crown him with many crowns*
Hail the day that sees him rise
Hail Redeemer, King divine*
King of glory, King of peace*
Let all the world*
New praises be given
Rejoice, the Lord is King*
The head that once was crowned*

Pentecost
Breathe on me, breath of God
Come down, O Love divine
Come, Holy Ghost, Creator, come
Holy Spirit, Lord of light
Veni, Creator Spiritus
Veni, sancte Spiritus

Trinity Sunday
Holy God, we praise thy name
Holy, holy, holy, Lord God almighty
Lead us, heavenly Father, lead us
Thou, whose almighty word

Corpus Christi
Let all mortal flesh
Of the glorious body telling
O thou, who at thy eucharist
Pange lingua gloriosi
Ubi caritas
Where is love and loving kindness

Blessed Virgin Mary
Ave maris stella
Holy light on God's horizon
Maiden yet a mother
Mary Immaculate, star of the morning
O Mary, of all women
Sing of Mary, pure and holy
Star of sea and ocean
Ye who own the faith of Jesus